UNCIVIL SOCIETY

UNCIVIL SOCIETY

GOVERNMENT'S WAR AGAINST GOD AND THE PLIGHT OF THE CHRISTIAN CITIZEN

ADAM MERSEREAU

BRIDGE
LOGOS
FOUNDATION

Alachua, Florida 32615

Bridge-Logos
Alachua, FL 32615 USA

Uncivil Society
Government's War Against God and the Plight of the Christian Citizen
by Adam Mersereau

Edited by Harold J. Chadwick

Printed in the United States of America.

Library of Congress Catalog Card Number: 2009944081
International Standard Book Number 978-0-88270-426-5

TO GRAMPS.

Contents

Preface

The world is changing, and America is changing with it. Americans have witnessed changes in their society that many of them could not have envisioned only fifty years ago. Some of those changes are dividing Americans. Not long ago, abortion was an unmentionable taboo in America. Today, many Americans believe it is a powerful symbol of women's liberation and a practical means of managing an unwieldy population. Roughly one half believe it is a constitutional right. For most of American history, Americans believed traditional marriage to be the foundation of a strong society; but today many believe restricting marriage to "one man and one woman" amounts to bigotry. Americans are increasingly divided also on the value of capitalism, the teaching of evolution, national healthcare, and the war on terror. Some view America as the "last best hope of earth." Others believe America—and perhaps all of Western civilization—was built upon a dubious value system and is responsible for a series of catastrophic failures that have tarnished human history.

There is a growing mood within the West that the West itself is a problem that must be solved. There is a deep sense of guilt that our narrow-mindedness and selfish individualism have left an embarrassing trail of imperialism, slavery, poverty, inequality, environmental harm, unnecessary wars, and social injustice. For many, this trail of woe overshadows the positive aspects of Western society. Some have concluded that the only solution is to remake the Western world and redefine its values.

But redefining Western values in some cases requires redefining biblical truths, because some of the most distinctive Western values are rooted in biblical teachings. This is particularly true for American values. In fact, the very foundations of freedom in America are built upon biblical truths. The duty of the individual to obey the law—even laws with which we disagree, and even when no one is watching—arises from the biblical revelation of a personal God who takes an interest in the personal holiness of individual people and prizes civil obedience. This individualized duty to obey the law, together with Christ's command that each person love his neighbor as himself, are the cornerstones of a free society, and both come from the Bible. The idea that all men should be treated equally under the law arises from the biblical teaching that all men are created in the image of God. The ideas that government power should be carefully limited and its various powers separated, arise from the biblical doctrine of original sin—the Fall of Man. The "separation of Church and state" is also a uniquely biblical teaching summarized in Jesus' famous exhortation to render unto Caesar that which is Caesar's.

For those who seek to remake Western society, however, biblical truth often presents obstacles. Nearly everyone can agree that we should love our neighbors, but other biblical teachings can be divisive. In a culture that yearns to be "progressive," biblical morality is too confining and biblical doctrine too dogmatic. If Western man is to be liberated from the parochial constraints that have produced the current state of human suffering, inequality, and injustice, and if Western society is to be re-imagined, some of God's laws as presented in the Bible must be overturned and rewritten. A new authority must be established that is big enough and powerful enough to topple the old value system and to enforce a new one.

Government—a large and powerful government filled with well-intentioned visionaries—is the key. To make room for this new all-powerful earthly authority, the biblical God must be disinvited from civil society. He may be allowed to rule within the four walls of the church, or privately at the dinner table, but He must have little influence over government.

The average man who supports the new vision for a new government and a new value system is sincere and compassionate. Unfortunately, his cause often leads him to embrace government policies that treat his neighbor not as an individual created in God's image, but as an integer in a larger equation. He sees a poor man in the street and he is saddened and stirred. He wonders "what can I do to help this man?" This is a good thought that all men should act upon to the best of their ability. He may also support public policies that will increase prosperity or provide a safety net for the less fortunate. But if he does not have a full understanding of the Fall of Man, he may lurch to the conclusion that the poor man could be poor only because of the inherent unfairness of Western society. The culprits, then, are Western values and Western capitalism. Suddenly, poverty seems easily preventable. His compassion sours into indignation. The poor man's individual need becomes less of an issue. His need becomes a symptom of a larger problem. The first question, "What can I do to help this man?" becomes "What can my government do to end all poverty?"

This desire—the desire to raise a government that can transform society—is the seed of utopianism, a temptation that has charmed mankind since the Garden of Eden. Utopianism is alive and well in the West and is surging in America. On any given day in America, you may hear the call to "cultural renewal" or "societal transformation" from the politician or from the pulpit. Some utopianists are secularists, and some are religious, but utopianism in general is on the rise.

Unfortunately, mobilizing society to fulfill the utopian vision always requires coercion by an increasingly powerful government. And with each increase in the power of government there is always an equal and opposite reduction in the rights of the individual. In his plans to reshape all of society, the utopian must transfer vast amounts of money and resources, he must pass sweeping legislation, and he must group society by impersonal statistical data: race, sex, income, age, education. In this way, the individual citizen is reduced to an integer in a larger equation. His individual rights become expendable for the greater good. The poor man on the street becomes a means to an end. This is how government power gets out of control, even in democracies. When the citizenry denies biblical truth—particularly the doctrine of the

Fall—the dream of utopia seems achievable; and when society adopts a utopian vision, tyranny creeps in.

In a fallen world, mankind is in a defensive posture toward sin and depravity. He cannot destroy it, he cannot defeat it. His challenge is to be holy in a fallen world, and to help alleviate the suffering of his neighbor—for he has the authority and ability to marshal his own resources for the benefit of his neighbor. But when the Fall is denied, the dream of utopia comes alive. The command to "love your neighbor" seems too quaint and is upgraded to "love your neighborhood." One must marshal the resources of others to benefit the entire neighborhood, and this requires putting undue faith in government.

Across the Western world, even in America, government now competes with God as an object of faith. Whether they realize it or not, those who place too much faith in government become foot soldiers in the cosmic revolt that mankind is waging against the authority of God. No one can serve two masters.

Amidst this whirlwind stands the Christian, asking "What is the biblical role of government? And what is my duty as a citizen in a society that appears to be in decline?" Fortunately, the Bible contains helpful answers. To understand them, we will start at the beginning—the Fall of Man in the Garden of Eden. For it is there that we learn the basics about the purpose of government, the essence of government, and the ever-present utopian urge. Then we will examine the Bible's teachings on the separation of Church and state and God's design for government in a fallen and largely non-Christian world. Once we understand God's design for government, we will discuss how mankind is laboring to deconstruct that design and replace it with his own. Using the examples of collectivism, abortion rights, and gay marriage, we will see how mankind is using government to challenge God's law and His authority. Lastly, we will look at the plight of the Christian citizen—how he must seek to live in a world turned upside down. Before we delve into the biblical view of government, however, we must understand the environment in which the Christian citizen now lives. In Part I, we will analyze the West's rejection of absolute truth, a development that makes it harder for Christians— who love truth—to gain a foothold in the public arena.

Some may conclude this book is pessimistic. If that is your conclusion, you have missed the point. The Western world is indeed in decline, but the Christian can take heart, because God's truth is eternal and immutable. And by God's sovereign design, the harder mankind toils to extinguish the light of God's truth, the brighter it shines for those who dare to apprehend it.

PART I

This Present Evil Age

WHY DO THE NATIONS RAGE

AND THE PEOPLES PLOT IN VAIN?

THE KINGS OF THE EARTH SET THEMSELVES,

AND THE RULERS TAKE COUNSEL TOGETHER,

AGAINST THE LORD AND AGAINST HIS

ANOINTED, SAYING,

"LET US BURST THEIR BONDS APART

AND CAST AWAY THEIR CORDS FROM US."

PSALM 2:1-3

CHAPTER 1

The West's Rejection of Truth

Imagine for a moment a world without Christianity. If that is too difficult, then imagine that Christ has not yet been born in Bethlehem. If that is still too difficult, suppose that Christ's teachings had never spread beyond a small group of His faithful followers in Palestine. Regardless of how you do it, take a moment to close your eyes and imagine that the world knows little or nothing about the Bible, the Gospel, and the teachings of Christ. Then ask yourself: Would the West be different? Would America be different?

In America today, children are taught in public schools that the founders of our nation were deists and rationalists who built America upon secular precepts as opposed to Christian truths. So we tend to believe that an America without Christianity would be much the same, and that the general course of Western history would be very similar. People would marry, have children, buy homes, seek education, work for a living, and save for retirement. People would naturally seek to improve their society through science, education, and a reasonable government that respects the dignity of all people. In our increasingly secular society, many no doubt believe the world would be better off without Christianity, and that it has been the source of much pain and suffering: the Crusades, the Inquisitions, Western imperialism, and the like.

Actually, our lives would be very different. Some historians, such as Paul Johnson, are bold enough to acknowledge that a world without Christianity would be a terrible place:

> Certainly, mankind *without* Christianity conjures up a dismal prospect. The record of mankind *with* Christianity is daunting enough.... The dynamism it has unleashed has brought massacre, torture, intolerance and destructive pride on a huge scale, for there is a cruel and pitiless nature in man which is sometimes impervious to Christian restraints and encouragements. But without these restraints, bereft of these encouragements, how much more horrific the history of these last 2,000 years would have been!... In the last generation, with public Christianity in headlong retreat, we have caught our first, distant view of a de-Christianized world, and it is not encouraging.[1]

Mr. Johnson could have gone much further. If you live in the West or in any nation whose culture has been shaped by Western values, your life would be very different without Christianity. All of the essential components of Western civilization are based upon biblical truths. The West would not be the West without the deep and abiding influence of the Christian faith. In ancient times, the

Western world was just as barbaric as any other civilization, and more so than some. But when Christianity spread to the Roman Empire in the First Century A.D., the Western world began to change dramatically.

Christian doctrine gave oxygen to the fledgling idea of Greek democracy: that individual citizens might participate in the selection of their rulers. Christianity bolstered the Roman idea that men should be governed by laws, not by other men. In other words, Christianity gave life to the principles that gave rise to the free societies of the Western world.

Eventually, the West spawned the United States of America, which became perhaps the most Western of all Western nations. It was founded on a distilled set of Western ideas that were rooted in biblical truths: that God creates all men personally and individually, meaning that any legitimate government must recognize the fundamental equality of all men before Him; that the affairs of men are guided by the hand of Providence, meaning that government is not the highest authority in the lives of its citizens; that the natural corruption of the human heart (original sin) behooves us to place checks and balances on governmental power; that it is best for all people, even rulers, to be subject to the rule of law; that government should protect all religions, leaving a man's conscience free to seek God as he thinks best, rather than constraining the religious urge by tyrannical decree or by force; and that the maintenance of justice requires the freedom of the people to participate in the selection of their rulers, to assemble, and to speak freely, even against those in power.

In other words, every important aspect of Western society, and particularly American society, is rooted in a biblical truth. It could never be otherwise. The idea of limited government would be a foolish idea if it were not necessitated by the reality of original sin. The idea that all men are created equal is an absurdity apart from a personal Creator who endows each individual with inherent worth and dignity equal to all others. The idea of freedom itself would be the most reckless and dangerous of ideas if people were not committed to self-governance in accordance with a moral law, and if they did not believe in a sovereign Providence that would guide their affairs.

If you stop for a moment to think about it, the principles of freedom could not have arisen from any other source. While our children are taught in public schools that such principles arose from human reason alone, this is a treacherous thought. If our fundamental rights are merely the product of secular human reason, then they can be simply reasoned away. The creation-story of the secular humanists (evolution), cannot account for the existence of eternal truths on which anyone's rights could be based. Without knowable, eternal truth, no one's rights would be unalienable, and we would have to deem the writers of the Declaration of Independence to have been either liars or delusional. Fortunately, America's founders understood that if mankind possessed any unalienable rights at all, they must come from God. As Alexis de Tocqueville put it, "Liberty regards religion as its companion in all its battles and its triumphs—as the cradle of its infancy, and the divine source of its claims. It considers religion as the safeguard of morality, and morality as the best security of law, and the surest pledge of the duration of freedom."[2]

4

Christianity is Foundational to Freedom

Yet, if we concede that freedom is rooted in a belief in God, must it be the Christian God? Could our freedom have arisen from the general principles of another religion, such as Islam? No. Only Christianity includes the doctrine of original sin, which is foundational to freedom. Islam is no exception. Islam teaches that man is inherently good, so Islam can provide no justification for limited government or the need for separate powers. In fact, the Muslim religion requires a strict system of theocracy based on "sharia" law, which is antithetical to democracy and to individual freedom. Oliver Roy, a French expert on Islam, observes, "Islam has not produced its own political model, economic system, autonomous public institutions, division between the family and the state, equal rights for women, or [any] community of states [outside of Muslim nations]."[3]

The principles underlying freedom could not come from Buddhism, either. The central teaching of Buddhism is that the existence of the "self" is an illusion. The practice of Buddhism is the practice of using various techniques to reach "nirvana," the perfect state of nothingness and non-perception. Thus the whole focus of Buddhism is to disabuse its adherents of all personal consciousness. It could never provide a basis for individual freedoms.

Hinduism provides no scope for political freedom, either. In many ways the precursor to Buddhism, Hinduism teaches that ultimate reality (Brahman) is an impersonal oneness in which there are no true personal or moral distinctions. Under Hinduism, the law of karma actually punishes people for seeking individual consciousness. In addition, their doctrine of reincarnation leads to an oppressive social structure, known in India as the caste system.[4] Like Buddhism, the goal of Hinduism is to lose your personal identity and be subsumed in the "universal self."

A review of all other religions yields the same result. Christianity provides the only possible foundations for a free society. The uniquely Christian doctrine of "Individualism" (i.e., that all individuals are created in the image of God, and are therefore of infinite significance and value) was one of the sparks that ignited Western freedom and provided the foundation for a democratic society. We will discuss Individualism in more detail in Chapter 7, but for now, suffice it to say that Christian Individualism had an enormous impact on Western democracy and freedom. Marcello Pera, an accomplished philosopher who later served as President of the Italian Senate, and who is not a believing Christian, put it this way:

> It is true that almost all of the achievements that we consider most laudable are derived from Christianity or were influenced by Christianity, by the message of God become Man. In truth, without this message, which has transformed all human beings into persons in the image of God, individuals would have no dignity. In truth, our values, rights and duties of equality, tolerance, respect, solidarity, and compassion are born from God's sacrifice. In truth, our attitude toward others, toward all others, whatever their condition, class, appearance, or culture is shaped by the Christian revolution. In truth, even our institutions are inspired by Christianity, including

the secular institutions of government that render under Caesar that which is Caesar's. And the list goes on.

Dismantling Our Own Foundations

It is no secret, however, that the West has largely rejected its Christian heritage. Today, the West is in the process of dismantling its own foundations. Western historians are reinventing Western history by deleting all references to Christianity. Even some Americans are turning away from the very foundations of freedom. Consider these opposing quotes, one by the second President of the United States, one by the man who became the forty-fourth President:

> The general principles upon which the Fathers achieved independence were the general principles of Christianity.... I will avow that I believed and now believe that those general principles of Christianity are as eternal and immutable as the existence and the attributes of God. (John Adams, Letter to Thomas Jefferson, 1813)

> It's not just absolute power that the Founders sought to prevent. Implicit in its structure, in the very idea of ordered liberty, was a rejection of absolute truth, the infallibility of any idea or ideology or theology.... (Barack Obama, *The Audacity of Hope*, 2006)

Many mighty civilizations have risen and fallen, but the world has never seen a civilization turn on its own foundations with such fervor. By its denial of absolute truth and its rejection of Christianity, the Western world has rejected the very source of the freedoms upon which it is built. It continues to lumber along primarily by force of habit. Its traditional institutions remain standing, but they are wobbly: marriage, the family, a form of the Church, and a relatively free economic system. Unless God intervenes in a very powerful and specific manner to revive it, it seems reasonable to anticipate a steady decline.

The decline of the West, including America, is cause for celebration in some parts of the world. It is even cause for celebration among many Westerners and Americans. Many see the downfall of the Western world as just deserts for its past colonization and subsequent abandonment of those colonies. "White Western guilt," as Shelby Steele has called it, is a powerful force in the West today. Westerners who do not believe in the absolute truths upon which Western civilization was founded cannot find any basis for the explosive prosperity of the West when compared to other civilizations. Because they believe Western truths are no better than any other cultures' "truths," they cannot account for the relative failure of other societies. The only logical conclusion is that the success of the West must have come at the expense of the rest of the world, most notably at the expense of the West's former colonies. This leads to a pervasive guilt for Western prosperity, and a controlling shame of the Western values that supposedly have caused such misery throughout the world.

It should be understood that the stain of imperialism cannot, and should not, be forgotten or repeated. Today, even the most loyal Westerner will agree. One could scour the Western world and not find a single credible advocate of future Western imperialism. To its credit, the West has long since rejected all notions of imperialism.

The Imperialism of Truth

Still, many Westerners harbor contempt for the West because it continues to commit what they view as a new kind of imperialism. This new imperialism is widely regarded as an unforgiveable sin: it is the belief that the truths upon which Western culture is based are true for all men. In today's world, in which absolute truth has been rejected, this is unthinkable. Samuel P. Huntington gave voice to the growing self-loathing of Westerners: "In the emerging world of ethnic conflict and civilizational clash, Western belief in the universality of Western culture suffers three problems: it is false; it is immoral; and it is dangerous."[5]

Much of the scorn aimed at the West is not actually scorn for the West, so much as it is scorn for the notion of absolute truth. Those who want to destroy the notion of absolute truth naturally find themselves attacking the biblical truths that are aligned with many tenets of Western civilization. To them, to attack the West is to attack Christianity, and to attack Christianity is to attack the West. And to attack either will accomplish their real purpose: to destroy the widely held Western belief in the existence of absolute truth.

The specter of deconstruction now looms over the Western world. To the deconstructionist, the very idea that traditional biblical principles might contain truths that are true for all men is oppressive, limiting, judgmental, discriminatory, and outdated. Thus, they desire to transform the West, and especially America, into a post-modern (or post Judeo-Christian) society in which almost all traditional values and morality are reduced to personal preferences, rendering it nonsensical to extend them beyond one's self.

Because Western civilization and its values are so closely aligned with biblical truths, the deconstructionists find it necessary to discredit them both. Yet, as mentioned earlier, Western civilization is founded on the idea that many biblical truths—and the Western values that spring from them—are indeed true for all men. America's founders, for example, believed that these biblical truths were not true only for them or their kind, but for all people. This meant that, for the first time in the history of the world, one nation would be built in which citizenship was determined primarily by allegiance to the truths identified in its founding documents. In other words, because these truths were held true for everyone, American citizenship would be available to anyone. (Even though the application of those truths was sometimes defective, such as in the case of the slaves, the truths themselves proved larger than the flawed men who penned them.)

Modern Liberals Embrace Deconstruction

Deconstructionists are not at home in Conservative circles, so they naturally gravitate toward Liberalism. Once we understand the goal of the deconstructionist, we begin to understand some of the inconsistencies in modern Liberalism. Modern Liberals stand firmly for the rights of women and minorities. Yet Liberals often seem to forget themselves when a successful woman or minority holds conservative views. Sadly, this is because such success stories do not echo the desired narrative of Liberalism: that Western culture and Western values are inherently oppressive to women and minorities. Conservative women and minorities who affirm Western values and who credit them for their success are harmful to the deconstructionist cause.

Understanding the goal of the deconstructionist also helps us understand the Liberal's affinity for socialism and communism. The Soviet Union, for example, was unashamedly founded on principles quite opposite to those of Western civilization, and particularly those on which America was founded. So long as the Soviet Union appeared strong and robust, it seemed to provide a constant reminder that Western values were not true for everyone, and that mankind could indeed find another way to organize a just and productive civilization. Those were the glory days for the deconstructionists. They reveled in the apparent success of the Soviet Union and made it their mission to praise Soviet communism and downplay its obvious flaws. For as long as the Soviet Union appeared powerful and healthy, their case against the universality of Western values seemed credible.

The strategy of elevating non-Western civilizations to make Western civilization appear less unique led directly to the "multiculturalism" movement. Going beyond the mere study of other cultures, multiculturalism seeks to indoctrinate people with the notion that all cultural systems are equally valid. This helps deconstructionists promulgate their claims against Western civilization.

After all, if the non-Western world is thriving without Western values, those Western values cannot possibly be rooted in eternal truths. To elevate other cultures, the multiculturalists inevitably must strain to articulate the beauty of many cultures that are not so beautiful—some in which children were sacrificed, in which violence is a way of life, in which discrimination is systematic, in which women are treated as property, and in which tyranny, ignorance, and occultism have resulted in great human suffering. The more wonderful and lovely other cultures appear, the smaller and less significant traditional Western values appear (and the truths upon which they rest). This is the multiculturalists' agenda.

In their efforts to discredit Western civilization and its values, the deconstructionists must not only downplay the failures of other civilizations, they must exaggerate the failures of our own. Some Americans are grateful for their Judeo-Christian heritage, but the deconstructionists look at American history and see mostly religious oppression, imperialism, and bigotry. Others might be inspired by the great sacrifices made by Americans to eradicate slavery, but the deconstructionists cannot see past the injustice of slavery, upon which, they claim, America was founded. Still other Americans might be grateful for the advancements spurred by free enterprise, but the deconstructionists see only poverty and environmental destruction.

All of this was on display in the recent international disputes over the War in Iraq. Although there were legitimate grounds upon which to oppose the invasion of Iraq—a fact which cannot be overstated—much of the opposition seemed surprisingly nonsensical. Some if it seemed aimed not at the war, but at America and the West in general. Why did the Iraq War stir so much anger and disdain for America and the West beyond rational disagreement with the war? Perhaps it was because something besides the Iraq War was at stake. If traditional Western values of governance ultimately provided the basis for a strong, peaceful, and free Iraq, then the world might see that much of what was true for 18th century white European Christian colonists is also true for 21st century Muslim Iraqis. Thus, the universality of Western values—and of the biblical truths that form the foundations of those values—would gain profound credibility. For deconstructionists seeking to discredit Western values, a Western victory in Iraq would be a setback. And so legitimate opposition to the Iraq War become mixed with a general scorn for the West and Western values.

Understand the Environment—
Know Where You Stand

What does all of this mean to today's Christian? We need to understand that the myriad attacks on the West and Western values are often attacks on the idea of absolute truth, and thus they are attacks on biblical truths as well. For example, as we will discuss in Part III, many Christians seem unaware that the idea of an absolute separation of Church and state is actually a frontal assault on God's sovereignty; that attacks against the sanctity of life often represent attacks on the idea of God as the creator of babies in the womb; and that the attack on traditional marriage is an attack on God's plan for human relationships and on His authority to place limits on those whom He has created.

Sadly, many in the Christian Church in America seem caught up in the anti-Western zeitgeist. To the extent their rejection of Western culture is a rejection of its materialism, sensuality, anti-intellectualism, and youth culture, this is entirely understandable. But Christians need to understand that the anti-Western spirit of the age is not always a rebellion against the West's many faults, but against its alignment with biblical truth. As churches strive to stay relevant, they must take care that that their anti-Western posture does not go too far. When Christian leaders are too eager to disassociate with Western values, they might begin to acquiesce in the fight for truth and inadvertently abandon biblical imperatives. When Christians become so concerned about the opinions of the world, they may forget who they are, they may lose their love for the truth, and they can become unable to take a stand when it really counts.

Truth is out of fashion in the West. Uncertainty in all things is the new mark of sophistication. So ashamed are we of the very concept of truth that we find ourselves censoring or re-interpreting the words of our forefathers, disassociating ourselves from them, because they often spoke unequivocally on matters of truth and religion. But because truth—particularly Christian truth—is foundational to Western society, the West is actually deconstructing the very foundations upon which it stands. Where to go from here?

ENDNOTES

1 Robert H. Bork, *Slouching Towards Gomorrah: Modern Liberalism and American Decline*, Regan Books, New York: 1996; p. 295 (quoting Paul Johnson, A History of Christianity (Simon and Schuster, New York: 1976; p. 517)).

2 Alexis de Tocqueville, Democracy in America, p. 48.

3 Oliver Roy, *The Failure of Political Islam*, trans. Carol Volk. Cambridge: Harvard University Press, 1996, p. 9; as quoted in Without Roots.

4 The formal caste system has been outlawed in India, but it remains part of the culture.

5 Samuel P. Huntington, *The Clash of Civilizations and the Remaking of the World Order*, New York, Simon and Schuster: 1998, p. 310.

★ CHAPTER 2 ★

The Futile Search for a Truthless Morality

Once the notion of absolute truth was widely discredited in the West, the landscape of politics and government began to change. The nature of public discourse had to change. The old ideas of truth and morality had to be replaced. In this new environment a new civil threat emerged. The new evil—the new unforgiveable sin—is to bring one's personal beliefs to bear in the arena of public policy.

Today, the moment that a Christian begins to think about the biblical role of government, and about his personal role as a citizen, a difficult question arises. Is it fair for Christians to insert their personal beliefs into a discussion about public affairs? The prevailing wisdom is that to bring one's personal beliefs to bear on matters of law and public policy is un-American. Good Americans, it is believed, are those who consciously set aside their personal beliefs and support laws that are "morally neutral."

Before we begin our study of the biblical view of government, we must address this concern. As we will see, despite the prevailing wisdom, there is no such thing as a law that is morally neutral, and the push for moral neutrality is not as benign as it may seem. Christians need to understand that the wisdom of mankind is not always very wise, and that being a good citizen does not always require us to set aside our beliefs before entering the public square.

The Fallacy of Neutrality

There is a man we all know. He is a well educated man who has made something of himself, probably more than you have made of yourself, in fact, and he is well aware of it. He loves to converse on politics and religion. At least, he believes he does. What he really loves is to hear himself speak of politics and religion while others listen. When he asks your opinion about a political or religious matter, he anticipates your answer before you give it and begins to declare his response to his own question, which he is quite sure is better than yours would be anyway.

This man, although an otherwise affable fellow, becomes particularly annoyed when the topic of Christianity arises. He is annoyed with Christians because he has only one enemy: dogmatism. He cannot tolerate the idea that any group of people, especially those who bow to the authority of an ancient book, might try to use the legislative process or court system to "force their beliefs" onto others. He despises this tendency among his Christian acquaintances and has vowed never to do it himself. He fancies himself a man of freedom, a man of free choice; and he considers himself far above the silly religious dogma that so often ensnares the narrow-minded.

Our affable friend has fully embraced the newest and most sacred principle upon which all of modern American politics now rests: that a true American should never insist that the law reflect his own personal beliefs about morality. This principle has been accepted by liberals and libertarians alike, and has become the irreducible and universal principle on which rests our entire system of government. In fact, in the minds of many Americans, adherence to this principle is what makes an American a "good American." When an American supports a law because it reflects his personal beliefs, he has committed what is perhaps the last remaining sin recognized in American popular culture. He is said to be guilty of forcing his beliefs onto others. He is a bad American.

This idea has the full support and blessing of the most powerful legal body in America, the United States Supreme Court. In *Planned Parenthood v. Casey*, a decision upholding abortion rights, the Court asserted:

> Some of us as individuals find abortion offensive to our most basic principles of morality, *but that cannot control our decision. Our obligation is to define the liberty of all, not to mandate our own moral code....* At the heart of liberty is the right to define one's own concept of existence, of meaning, of the universe, and of the mystery of human life."[1]

Similarly, in *Lawrence v. Texas*, a decision that favored the rights of gays to be married, the Court argued:

The condemnation [of homosexual conduct as immoral] has been shaped by religious beliefs, conceptions of right and acceptable behavior, and respect for the traditional family. For many persons these are not trivial concerns but profound and deep convictions accepted as ethical and moral principles to which they aspire and thus determine the course of their lives. *These considerations do not answer the question before us, however. The issue is whether the majority may use the power of the State to enforce those views on the whole society through the operation of criminal law. Our obligation is to define the liberty of all, not to mandate our own moral code.*[2]

The Supreme Court has inserted a bright line between private morality and good public policy. It does at first seem (doesn't it?) that Christians are sometimes faced with a dilemma. Should they seek to force Christian morality onto others, or should they support morally neutral laws that allow individuals to define good and evil for themselves? Should Christians force their views about abortion onto others, or should they support morally neutral laws that allow people to decide for themselves? Should Christians force their views about marriage onto others, or should they support morally neutral laws that allow homosexuals to marry?[3]

As it turns out, this is a false choice. No law and no decision by any court is morally neutral, not even a law that is pro-choice on abortion, and not even a law that allows homosexuals to marry. Every time the government promulgates a law or refuses to promulgate one, it makes a moral judgment, because all laws either encourage or discourage certain behavior. Judges and legislators can distinguish between desirable and undesirable behavior only by borrowing a moral principle from one belief system or another. So, every time a new law comes before a legislature, the debate is really over whose belief system—whose morality—the law will reflect. To prove this point, we will examine the two controversial issues addressed by the Supreme Court in the passages above: abortion rights and gay marriage. But first, it may be helpful to look at an example of a very uncontroversial law that is commonly believed to be morally neutral.

Aren't Civil Rights Laws Morally Neutral?

The Civil Rights Act of 1964 has become the archetypal law in America. It is supposedly the perfect example of a law that is morally neutral. By banishing all personal beliefs about race from the public square, it is believed, the Civil Rights Act creates a bias-free legal system in which people of all races and creeds can co-exist in harmony.[4]

Prior to the Civil Rights Act, some of our laws were racially discriminatory because they reflected a belief system in which God had endowed whites with more dignity than blacks. But the Civil Rights Act, and the bold movement that produced it, forced courts and lawmakers to cleanse the law of racial bias. This would promote racial neutrality in our laws and public policies. But racial neutrality is not the same thing as moral neutrality.

The Civil Rights movement was not a morally neutral movement, and the laws it yielded are not morally neutral laws. The Civil Rights movement challenged the racist belief system with yet another belief system: that God created white and non-white people in His own image, that He loves them equally, and that people of all races are therefore endowed with equal dignity. Like all struggles for the law, this was a struggle over which belief system (racist or non-racist) should be reflected in the law. But Civil Rights laws are anything but morally neutral. In fact, the last thing a citizen would ever want is a government that is morally neutral on the value and dignity of human beings. If the government were in fact morally neutral on this issue, then it would be equally lax—not equally diligent—in its protection of people's civil rights. No one's rights would be protected.

To be truly dispassionate on racial issues, then, our lawmakers and judges must be extremely passionate proponents of a particular belief system under which people of all races are possessed of equal dignity. To support laws that reflect this belief system is certainly a mark of a good citizen—a good American—but it is not morally neutral. This is a critical point to understand because it shows us that the most powerful and unifying legislation passed by Congress in recent history, which seems to be entirely neutral of morality, is actually based on a profound moral belief.

Now, using the same method we have used to examine the Civil Rights Act, we will look at two more controversial examples of laws that are thought to be morally neutral: those governing abortion and those that would allow homosexuals to marry. Although these laws allow "free choice," we will see they, too, represent strong moral statements.

Aren't Pro-Choice Laws Morally Neutral?

Many Americans seem to agree that our laws are morally neutral on abortion. In *Roe v. Wade* (and several subsequent decisions), the Supreme Court essentially recused itself and the rest of the government from influencing a mother's moral judgment on whether the fetus in her womb should be treated as a "person" or not. Many Americans applaud this ruling because they believe that before *Roe v. Wade*, the law discriminated against women by denying them the right to make the decision for themselves. By leaving the decision entirely to the mother, it appears the government has taken a hands-off approach. This is the way many Americans like it.

But the government's approach to abortion is not morally neutral. By leaving the decision to the mother, the government adopts a particular belief system about the value and dignity—or lack thereof—of the unborn. Think of it this way: the only other time our laws allow private citizens to choose life or death (for an innocent life) is in the case of non-endangered wildlife. Citizens are allowed to choose at their whim, for example, whether to hunt and kill deer, ducks, geese, and pheasants during hunting season; whether to release a garden snake back into the garden or chop off its head with a spade; whether to flush a spider down the toilet or toss it out the door to live another day. Some people's consciences don't allow them to kill these creatures, while others don't think twice. Our attitudes turn on our personal beliefs about the value and dignity of animals, a question upon which reasonable minds can differ.

By leaving these life-or-death decisions to the individual, our courts and legislatures have imposed a particular belief system onto animals and the people who love them: animals are less valuable than humans are, and thus do not warrant the same protections. You may agree or disagree with this position, but there is no doubt that the government has made a moral judgment on the value and dignity of wildlife.

Similarly, by allowing an expectant mother to make the life-or-death decision for her unborn child, the government also makes a moral judgment: a fetus is less than human and does not warrant the same protections. In other words, when the government places the unborn into the same category as a goose in hunting season— rather than in the category with other human beings— the government is adopting a particular belief system. It is not morally neutral. Government may not be making the ultimate decision whether to abort a pregnancy (just as it does not dictate that you flush the spider); but the business of categorizing an unborn child as human or something less is a moral business.

The debate over abortion, therefore, is not a debate about discrimination against women. It is linked to one's beliefs about the unborn. And the pro-choice position is not a morally neutral position because it demands that the law reflect a very specific set of beliefs regarding the humanity of unborn children.

Aren't Laws Allowing Gay Marriage Morally Neutral?

The debate over gay marriage is no different. For a very long time, mankind has more or less agreed that God established marriage as a union between one man and one woman. Human government certainly must recognize and regulate marriage, but no one believed government created marriage. Today, however, a new belief is on the rise—that marriage is man-made, merely a creation of the law, and can therefore be redefined by lawmakers or courts.

Once again, this is a debate over whose belief system will be reflected in the law. Judges and legislators in California, Massachusetts, and elsewhere may debate whether heterosexual marriage is the foundation of society, or whether children are best raised by a mom and dad. But all Americans need to understand what is really happening. The real struggle over gay marriage is a struggle between two belief systems with two different definitions of marriage. One holds that God gave us marriage between one man and one woman, and so we are not at liberty to redefine it; the other seeks to reduce marriage to a man-made creation that can be changed as the mood strikes.

For this reason, laws that give homosexuals the choice to marry are not morally neutral laws. Instead, such laws reflect a very particular and a very personal belief about the origins and nature of marriage. Like the abortion debate, the debate over gay marriage is not a struggle between moral dogmatism and moral neutrality; it is a struggle over whose moral dogmatism will be reflected in the law.

When Dogma Poses as Neutrality

This fallacy of neutrality is one of the most common aspects of modern American politics. We often hear politicians say, "Personally, I believe that abortion (or gay marriage) is wrong, but I do not believe my personal beliefs should become the law of the land." These kinds of statements not only reveal the fallacy of neutrality, they are also illogical. One's personal beliefs about right and wrong should always come from one's beliefs about what is true. For example, supporters of civil rights should support civil rights only if they believe God endowed people with equal dignity. If God has not so endowed people, it would make little sense to support civil rights. Likewise, opponents of civil rights should oppose civil rights only if they believe God did not endow all people with equal dignity. On what other reasonable grounds could civil rights possibly be opposed?

Similarly, pro-choicers should be pro-choice only if they believe a fetus is not human. If they believe a fetus is human and yet remain pro-choice, they embrace a policy that is evil beyond imagination. Pro-lifers should be pro-life only if they believe a fetus is human. If they are pro-life for another reason, they must contend with the rights of the mother. Supporters of traditional marriage must believe traditional marriage is an eternal truth; and supporters of gay marriage should believe marriage is man-made if their position is to be logically coherent.

When a politician severs his personal beliefs on morality from laws that contain assumptions about morality, he forfeits rationality. In essence he is saying: "Personally, I believe abortion is wrong because I believe a fetus is human, but I also believe that the law should contain no protections for that particular class of humans;" or "Personally, I believe that it is wrong for the law to recognize the marriage of two men because I believe that traditional marriage is an eternal truth, but I also believe the law should treat marriage as if it were man-made and thus malleable to our liking." One may as well say, "Personally, I believe it is wrong to discriminate against blacks because blacks and whites are possessed of equal dignity, but I do not believe they should have equal rights under the law." This is, of course, nonsense.

For this reason, if you ever hear a politician from your district say, "Personally, I believe … is wrong, but …" you should run for the hills, for it is clear that (a) he holds personal beliefs that he knows are inconsistent with his convictions of what is true, or (b) he sees no need for the law to reflect the truth as he sees it, or (c) he does not completely believe what he says he believes, and is deceiving voters in order to sneak his own dogmatic beliefs into the game. Regardless of the reason for his statement, he should not be allowed near the law-making process.

Truth vs. Personal Preferences

Keep in mind that we are speaking here about matters of truth, not mere preferences. It is right and proper in a democracy for people to debate matters of truth and how they are reflected in the law. But obviously, in a pluralistic society like ours, the government should remain neutral on matters of personal taste. No one should fight to outlaw all colors but their own favorite color; nor all foods except their own favorite foods. Turkish delight may be your favorite food, but this is (clearly) a matter of opinion that is not true for all men. That a fetus is a human being, however, is either true for all men or not true at all. It cannot be true for one person and false for another. Green may be your favorite color, while your neighbor prefers blue. He cannot say you are wrong for loving green. But if the two of you differ on whether God created marriage or mankind created marriage, you have a problem. One of you is wrong. This is the difference between matters of preference or opinion, and matters of truth.

If the Law Were Morally Neutral, There Would Be No Duty to Obey It

If all truth is reduced to personal opinion, then truth does not exist (or as some would say, it cannot be known, which yields the same result). But if truth does not exist (or if it cannot be known), then the laws that govern society are devoid of truth. If the law is devoid of truth—devoid of morality—then it is nonsense to claim that citizens have a moral duty to obey it. And if there is no moral duty to obey the law, then the very foundation of a free and civil society is a sham.

The importance of this point cannot be overstated. Because in a free society the government has limited powers to dictate behavior, they rely heavily on the self-governance of the citizenry. The people must be relied upon to obey the laws without supervision in the daily course of life. Only the religious belief that man has a duty before God to obey the law can produce such a self-governing and thus free society. This is, of course, what led George Washington to say, "Of all the dispositions and habits which lead to political prosperity, religion and morality are indispensable supports."[5] It is also what led John Adams to say, "Our Constitution was made only for a moral and religious people. It is wholly inadequate to the government of any other."[6]

Those who believe truth is non-existent or unknowable can provide no philosophical basis for a free society. This has not stopped them from trying. For centuries, secular philosophers have tried desperately to cobble together a duty arising out of a "social contract" or a "natural duty."[7] And try they must, because they know if citizens are under no independent moral duty to obey the law, then lawlessness cannot be immoral. They are therefore desperate to find a duty somewhere, anywhere, because they fear that once the masses realize there is no God given duty, there will be chaos. To avoid this result, they must slowly and methodically gain control over the citizens. That is why the secularist worldview—one that denies the existence or knowability of truth—inevitably leads to larger government and more state control over daily life.

The lesson learned is this: Christians have every right to assert Christian beliefs in those public debates that concern matters of truth. Although there are biblical limits on which matters of truth are appropriate for the public realm (as we will discuss in later chapters), Christians need not remain silent for fear of forcing their beliefs onto others.

What is a vote, after all, if not an attempt to force one's beliefs onto others? Every time your neighbor casts a vote, he is trying to force his beliefs upon you. Every time you cast a vote, you are trying to force your beliefs upon him. To one degree or another, everyone is trying to force their beliefs onto others, and Christians should not be summarily sidelined under the twisted logic of the secularist. In fact, the entire movement in the Western world toward so-called moral neutrality is a ruse—it is a veil behind which the new man-made morality is kept hidden from view. Seen in the light of day, many would recognize it as evil. Cloaked in a seemingly benign veil of moral neutrality, it slips past the dulled conscience of a society in decline.

The business of law-making in a democracy is the business of fighting for laws that are just, and to be just, they must correspond to the truth. The Christian should be well equipped to engage in discussions about truth; but he must also be fully aware that truth has in many ways become an enemy to the world in which he lives.

ENDNOTES

1   *Planned Parenthood of Southeaster Pa. v. Casey*, 505 U.S. 833, 850-851 (1992) (emphasis added).

2   *Lawrence v. Texas*, __ U.S.__, 123 S. Ct. 2427, 2480 (2003) (quoting Casey, 505 U.S. at 850)(emphasis added).

3   There is, of course, no such thing as "gay marriage," because God created marriage to be between one man and one woman. The term "gay marriage" is used here only as shorthand.

4   The Civil Rights Act of 1964 outlawed discrimination on the basis of race, religion, gender, and ethnicity in public schools and other public places, and by employers. The driving force behind the Act, however, was to reduce discrimination against African-Americans.

5   Farewell Address.

6   October 11, 1798.

7   While their proponents seek to define a duty that is morally neutral, both theories rely on borrowed moral principles that are smuggled in to fill the gaps.

PART II

The Biblical View of Government

FOR THERE IS NO AUTHORITY EXCEPT FROM
GOD, AND THOSE THAT EXIST HAVE BEEN
INSTITUTED BY GOD.

ROMANS 13:1B

CHAPTER 3

Government and the Fall

L iving in a culture in which biblical truths are under constant assault can be very disorienting to Christians. Some Christians acquiesce easily and survive by retrofitting Christianity to the latest cultural trends. Others feel the weight of every cultural battle directly upon their shoulders and become embittered and angry. The goal of the Christian, however, should be to think and behave more like Christ our Savior. Christ came to Earth in human form and lived in an unjust Roman society that persecuted Christians, approved of slavery, oppressed women, and used tax revenues to fund pagan temples. Jesus clearly hated injustice and was not unfamiliar with righteous anger; yet, He was not embittered. In fact, He paid His taxes to the local government and to the corrupt authorities in the temple. What did Jesus know that we don't? What can we learn from the Bible about the proper role of government and the Christian's role in society?

In this chapter, our goal is to set aside for a moment the myriad cultural battles raging around us and understand what the Bible says about God, government, and Christian citizenship. We will examine the biblical view of government. In later chapters, we will look at the way mankind distorts it.

And you will be like God...

Have you ever walked alone through an unfamiliar forest with only a map and compass? Have you felt the awful feeling of being lost and alone? When lost, the only way to find your way is to calm yourself and figure out exactly where you are. This is true not only when navigating with a map and compass. It is also true in the search for truth. If we begin a search for truth from the wrong starting point, we will find not the truth, but error. And error begets error. So, in our search for the biblical view of government, we must begin at the proper starting place—the Fall of man as recorded in Genesis.

In the first chapters of Genesis, we read that God placed Adam in the Garden of Eden to work and take care of it. Adam was perfectly content. God had supplied him with everything he needed, and his relationship with God was personal and intimate. But God imposed on Adam one rule, or law, that Adam must obey: "And the LORD God commanded the man, saying, 'You may surely eat of every tree of the garden, but of the tree of the knowledge of good and evil you shall not eat, for in the day that you eat of it you shall surely die.'"[1] Later, God tasked Adam with naming the various animals and birds in the Garden. But Adam found none of them suitable helpers, so God created a wife for him, named Eve. Presumably, Adam informed his new wife about the law that God had given him regarding the tree of the knowledge of good and evil.

In Chapter 3 of Genesis, Satan appears in the form of a serpent and speaks to Eve. He zeroes in on the rule concerning the tree. Satan preys craftily upon any discontentment Adam and Eve might harbor about the prohibition God has placed on them. He asks, "Did God actually say, 'You shall not eat of any tree in the garden'?"[2] Notice that Satan misstates the law. God did not tell Adam he mustn't eat from any tree. To the contrary, God had provided Adam and Eve with many fruitful trees and bountiful provisions. He had forbidden Adam only from eating of one particular tree—the tree of the knowledge of good and evil.

Then, Eve responds, "We may eat of the fruit of the trees in the garden, but God said, 'You shall not eat of the fruit of the tree that is in the midst of the garden, neither shall you touch it, lest you die.'"[3] Eve's response is not completely accurate. While she defends God's general goodness by correcting Satan and assuring him that God has provided them plenty to eat, she does not entirely disagree with Satan. Satan had implied that God's rule was overly restrictive. Eve must have agreed to some extent because she also overstates the rule by saying that God forbade her and Adam from even "touching" the particular tree. But God never said they should not *touch* it, only that they should not *eat* of it. Sensing Eve's lack of certainty about God's intentions, Satan moves in for the kill. "You will not surely die," he tells her, "For God knows that when you eat of it your eyes will be opened, and you will be like God, knowing good and evil."[4]

Let's pause here for one moment. Why is the tree called "the tree of the knowledge of good and evil?"

We cannot be certain whether the tree was infused by God with magical power, or whether it was an ordinary tree. Either way, God used the fruit of the tree and the prohibition against eating it in a special way. Eating its fruit against God's command would expose Adam and Eve to a new kind of knowledge. Being in the Garden that God had made for them, knowing God intimately and having a proper relationship with Him, Adam and Eve to this point had knowledge only of the good. If they ate of the tree, however, they would have knowledge not only of the good, but of evil as well.

What is wrong with knowing both good and evil? Actually, it presents a huge problem. Only God can have knowledge of evil and yet never succumb to its temptations. For mankind to know evil is disastrous. It dramatically alters his nature and his relationships with God, his fellow man, the creation, and ultimately the very world in which he lives. Satan well understood the trap he was setting. Adam and Eve did not.

They ate the forbidden fruit, and they indeed acquired the knowledge of good and evil. The effects of acquiring such knowledge are illustrated in part by the immediate reaction of Adam and Eve after they ate the forbidden fruit. The Scripture says, "Then the eyes of both were opened, and they knew that they were naked."[5] In other words, they became self-aware. Before they ate the forbidden fruit, their hearts were fully aligned with God, His purity, and His purposes. Their relationship with their Creator was in proper perspective and they were not concerned with even their own nakedness. Nor did they view each other as objects. They could view each other, naked as they were, and see only a fellow child of God—just as God saw them.

But after eating the fruit, they hid their nakedness. They hid, not out of humility, but out of pride. In their fall, they had become too prideful to allow themselves to be seen as they really were. They had descended into the sin of narcissism. They could no longer stand to be seen— to be scrutinized—by each other, or by God. God became an outsider—a competitor for authority over the self. In short, God became an enemy.

Adam and Eve would not bear their sin alone. As the first and archetypal human beings, their actions were taken on behalf of their progeny, all of whom would henceforth be born into sin. Before they had their first child, Adam and Eve had become the parents of a sinful race. Just as God had warned Adam, from that day forward every human being would suffer the inescapable penalty of sin: death.

This raises the next logical question: Knowing this would happen, why did God place the tree of the knowledge of good and evil in the Garden in the first place? Why would God create a place of perfect peace and safety for Adam and Eve, establish an eternal and intimate fellowship with them, equip them with everything they needed for life and contentment, and then place a deathly tree in the middle of it? Why would He make so many fruitful trees for their nutrition and pleasure, and yet make one more, and attach to it a deadly prohibition? And why would He place it right in the middle of the Garden?

By placing the tree of the knowledge of good and evil into the middle of this heavenly Garden, God was laying down the law: for Adam and Eve to have a proper relationship with the Creator, they must fully trust God's judgment of what was best for them. The tree, standing in the middle of the Garden, was the perfect symbol of trust. As long as its fruit went uneaten, there could be no doubt that Adam and Eve were content to trust God's decisions for them. It meant they trusted His goodness. God was essentially saying, "I am God, and I have made you, and I have given you all you need. I have not withheld anything good from you. Whatever I have withheld from you, I have withheld because it is not good, but evil. You can trust my goodness and my plan for your life. This tree represents your trust in me and in my goodness. As long as you trust me, you will leave it alone. So it stands as a constant reminder and symbol of your trust. But it is more than a symbol. If you eat of it, you will have already decided that I am not trustworthy. You will have determined to overrule my goodness and to create your own. You will have broken trust with the only one who is truly trustworthy."

Satan knew the existence of the tree could be twisted into the perfect temptation. He would use the seeds of distrust to lure mankind away from God, and into his own miserable company. Adam and Eve would eat of the tree only if they could be persuaded that God was holding out on them. Had God really shown them all that was good? Was God hiding anything from them? Was there anything about this so-called evil that perhaps was not so evil? If they understood fully the basis for God's decisions, would they agree?

In the end, Adam and Eve could not stand the thought that God and God alone would get to decide what was truly good for them. They wanted to look behind the curtain. They wanted to be the deciders. They wanted to judge His decisions—to judge for themselves whether God was acting rightly or wrongly; whether He was truly good; and whether He was withholding some things that might benefit them. The implication is that, if Adam and Eve knew all that God knew, their decisions might very well differ from His. This desire to "be like God," to usurp His authority, is the essence of sin. At its core, sin is a rejection of God's goodness and a rebellion against the authority of God. It was the same visceral desire that led Satan and his clan of like-minded angels to rebel against God in heaven. They chose to break fellowship with God. They wanted to be their own rulers. They coveted God's authority.

The effects of sin are myriad, and many of them are beyond the scope of our topic. But we need to take note of a few essential lessons from the Fall:

• Sin is a deconstructive and parasitic force. It usually entails the distortion of God's revealed truth—just as Satan and then Adam and Eve twisted God's words to reach their desired result.

• The essence of sin is the rejection of God's authority to declare what is good and what is evil, and a prideful desire to make that determination for ourselves. Sin is rebelliousness leading to narcissism. It is the belief that if decisions of good and evil were left to mankind, mankind would make a much better world for himself. Sinful man believes he can create a better world than God has created (and which God has sovereignly allowed to remain in a fallen state for a period of time known only to Him). This is the humanistic dream of utopia, and it is nothing more than rebellion writ large across all of society.

The Purpose and Essence of Government [6]

At the end of Chapter 3 of Genesis, after cataloguing the curses to which all of mankind and all creation would now be subjected, we read, "Then the LORD God said, 'Behold, the man has become like one of us in knowing good and evil. Now, lest he reach out his hand and take also of the tree of life and eat, and live forever'—therefore the LORD God sent him out from the garden of Eden to work the ground from which he was taken. He drove out the man, and at the east of the garden of Eden he placed the cherubim and a flaming sword that turned every way to guard the way to the tree of life."[7]

Here we find clues to the purpose and essence of government. This is the first instance of God delegating the use of force—in this case to the sword-wielding cherubim—to restrain mankind. God's purpose for blocking Adam and Eve's reentry to the Garden was not only for their punishment, but also for their protection. They had become sinners by a fatal act of distrust, betrayal, and rebellion. God did not want them to dwell in the Garden where they might have access to the tree of life.[8] Here we find the very purpose of government and the very essence of government.

The purpose of government is to make laws that restrain evil by protecting mankind from the full effects of his own rebellion and lawlessness.

The essential aspect of government—the thing that makes the government the government—is the power to use force. Anyone can make a rule and call it a law. But when a person or group of persons has received the authority to make laws, and has the authority and power to enforce those laws, this is government.

The Depth and Breadth of the Fall

Before we conclude our review of the Fall and its impact on the proper role of government, we must pause to recognize the sheer depth and breadth of it. Adam was not an ordinary man. God created him to be the archetype, the federal head of all humanity, so that when Adam fell all of his progeny fell with him.[9] The *Westminster Confession*[10] explains, "Our first parents being the root of all mankind, the guilt of their sin was imputed, and the same death in sin and corrupted nature were conveyed to all their posterity, descending from them by ordinary generation." The revered Princeton theologian, Charles Hodge, expounds:

> It is both a doctrine of Scripture and fact of experience that mankind are a fallen race. Men universally, under all the circumstances of their being in this world, are sinful and exposed to innumerable evils. Many of these evils, and in many instances the most appalling, come upon the children of man in early infancy anterior to

any possible transgressions of their own. This is a fact which cannot be denied and for which the human mind has tortured itself to find a solution. The Scriptural solution of this fearful problem is that God constituted our first parent the federal head and representative of his race and placed him on probation not only for himself, but also for all his posterity.... [A]s he fell from the estate in which he was created, they fell with him in his first transgression, so that the penalty of that sin came upon them as well as upon him.[11]

By Chapter 4 of Genesis, the sin of jealousy led one of Adam's progeny, Cain, to murder his brother Abel,[12] and by Chapter 6 we are told that "the wickedness of man was great in the earth, and that every intention of the thoughts of his heart was only evil continually."[13] Thus began the downward spiral of humanity. The prophet Jeremiah tells us, "The heart is deceitful above all things, and desperately sick."[14] The Psalmist makes it clear that our depravity is congenital: "Behold, I was brought forth in iniquity, and in sin did my mother conceive me."[15] Charles Hodge observes further:

Not only do we see [in children] the manifestations of anger, malice, selfishness, envy, pride and other evil dispositions, but the whole development of the soul is toward the world. The soul of a child turns by an inward law from God to the creature, from the things that are unseen and eternal to the things that are seen and temporal. In its earliest manifestations it is worldly, of the earth, earthy....

"Foolishness (moral evil) is bound in the heart of the child" (Proverbs 22:15).[16]

Paul explains in Romans that, having been born into sin, mankind's controlling flaw is the suppression of God's truth.[17] In other words, God has made himself known, but mankind will not have it.[18] Mankind is fully aware of God, or has every reason to be, but still refuses to acknowledge God's Lordship. Refusing to give honor to Him or show thankfulness to Him, the human race "became futile in their thinking, and their foolish hearts were darkened. Claiming to be wise, they became fools, and exchanged the glory of the immortal God" for idols and lies.[19] For this reason, God actually gave mankind over to sin,[20] and the downward spiral has continued out of control until the present day. Because of his stubborn refusal to acknowledge the reality of God, even mankind's ability to reason properly has been tarnished.[21] Because of our insistent refusal to bend the knee to God, the Bible describes sinful man as being dead in sin, slaves to sin, and having hearts of stone.[22] In fact,

> None is righteous, no, not one; no one understands; no one seeks for God. All have turned aside; together they have become worthless; no one does good, not even one.[23]

Man rejects God's authority, His truth, and His goodness. Sin is rebellious, ungrateful, and incurable (apart from Christ). It causes man to seek his own aggrandizement, comfort, and security. It dominates the mind, the affections, and the will. It leads to death and to eternity in hell. Everyone is born in sin, and apart from Christ all men are willing servants to it. In summary, in the Fall, mankind turned against God and became His enemy.[24]

Obviously, not all men are as sinful as they could possibly be. Nor are all men equally sinful. Both Scripture and our common experience testify that sinful man, to varying degrees, can be "honest in dealings, kind in their feelings, and beneficent in their conduct."[25] God has indeed given each man a conscience that whispers the statutes of God to the inner man, and to varying degrees he may comply with those whispers, though he always does so with impure motives that are not to God's glory.[26] Unable to please God, even when acting in accordance with God's law, mankind's tainted obedience serves as a reminder of his helpless state, but it can do nothing to assuage God or reverse the effects of the Fall.

Like fishes born in water who do not know they are wet, all men are born into sin, suppressing the truth all the while, with no way out apart from the Cross of Christ. Good deeds cannot save us. Our heritage, whatever it may be, cannot save us. No ceremonial rite can save us. We cannot claim a lack of knowledge—for there is no excuse. All of these are lame substitutes for real salvation and real sanctification through Jesus Christ. But God cannot be deceived. There are no short-cuts and no safe harbors in which to escape the fact of our sinfulness or its penalties. Even when saved by the grace of God, Christians battle sin on a moment-by-moment basis, and must constantly draw on the power of the Holy Spirit to overcome even the most trivial seeming sins.

But that is not all. In addition to the Fall of mankind, all of creation was cursed as well. When God banished Adam and Eve from the Garden of Eden, He issued this judgment among the others:

> Because you have listened to the voice of your wife and have eaten of the tree of which I commanded you, "You shall not eat of it," cursed is the ground because of you; in pain you shall eat of it all the days of your life; thorns and thistles it shall bring forth for you; and you shall eat the plants of the field. By the sweat of your face you shall eat bread, till you return to the ground, for out of it you were taken; for you are dust, and to dust you shall return.[27]

God had provided abundantly, freely, and easily for Adam and Eve prior to the Fall. From the Fall forward, however, the Earth would be cursed and Adam's life would entail toil, sweat, frustration, and even futility. King Solomon in all his wisdom said of mankind's plight, "all his days are full of sorrow, and his work is a vexation."[28] Of mankind's plans, schemes, and general plight in the fallen world, Solomon exclaimed: "Vanity of vanities! All is vanity."[29] Paul observes that all of creation is in bondage to corruption, and that creation has been "groaning ... in the pains of childbirth"[30] as it awaits the final redemption. In fact, part of the cursing of the creation was that it was henceforth sentenced to catastrophic destruction at the end of the age. Peter tells us "the heavens and the earth that now exist are stored up for fire, being kept until the day of judgment and destruction of the ungodly."[31]

All of this, and we have not yet mentioned that the Fall brought death to mankind—spiritual and physical death. Recall that when God commanded Adam not to eat of the tree of the knowledge of good and evil, He warned them of the penalty of doing so. He said, "for in the day that you eat of it, you shall surely die." Thus, on the day they ate of the tree, Adam and Eve suffered spiritual death.[32] Later they would suffer physical death, as would all men after them. "To dust you shall return."[33] With the Fall came the inevitability of aging, suffering, disease, and ignoble death.

Your View of the Fall Will Determine Your View of Government

A person's view of the Fall (whether it really happened and the extent of its effects) will invariably determine his or her politics and view of government. It may well be the most significant fault line between modern liberalism and conservatism. Speaking in the most general terms (which can be treacherous), conservatives are those who lean toward the belief that government can mitigate the effects of the Fall; while liberals lean toward the view that government can reverse it (if it happened at all). Because the conservative is doubtful of what government can achieve in a fallen world, he is reluctant to trade his precious rights to empower it. Because the liberal is more optimistic about what government can accomplish, he is far more willing to sacrifice personal freedoms. To avoid the potential unfairness of using loaded terms such as *liberal* and *conservative*, however, consider how two hypothetical men on the street with two different views of the Fall might see the world.

One man believes the world is shipwrecked and cut off from all that is good and redemptive. The best he can do is cling heroically to those truths he knows are eternal, faithfully prepare for the day of rescue, and strive to live in a manner that gives others hope that the rescuer, Christ, has come, and will return again. Another man believes that the world is on the verge of perfection, but is held back from perfection only by a lack of imagination and self-sacrifice by his fellow man. If only they could be convinced to see it, they would have it.

The man who believes in the Fall—the comprehensive Fall as taught in the Bible, or something like it—sees the world as a tragic place. Above all, he is suspicious of his own plans and schemes, because he knows his own heart is sinful. When he looks into his heart, he is afraid of the darkness there, and he cries out to God for mercy and for wisdom to know the truth and to do what is right. His struggle is to fight the daily battle to overcome his sin, both in his private life and his public conduct. He is a cautious man. Not paranoid, but cautious. Because he knows mankind's heart is sinful, he is reluctant to trust fully in the plans and schemes of other men, especially of powerful men. Because he is deeply engaged in an individual struggle to overcome his sin, he views other people essentially as individuals, and he believes what defines them as such is how they confront or fail to confront their own sinfulness.

As he looks at the world around him and sees war, poverty, injustice, and oppression, he is saddened. But he seeks to set aside his sadness and to love his neighbor, as God commands him. He receives this command—this simple command to love his neighbor—as one of the secrets to survival in the fallen world. He recognizes that in the current fallen age, his personal power is limited. He cannot change the world, but in loving his neighbor, he can help alleviate the pain of the Fall. It is his quiet show of allegiance to God, his simple act of defiance against the Fall. To him, government is a temporary and necessary evil, established by God to preserve some semblance of order among fallen men and nations. He is not a pessimist about life on the whole, but is fairly pessimistic about government. He "has become accustomed to the idea that there is a deep interior dislocation in the very center of human personality, and that you can never, as they say, 'make people good by Act of Parliament.'"[34]

The man who does not believe in the biblical Fall sees the world very differently. He looks into his own heart and sees primarily good intentions, primarily honest desires. He will acknowledge his obvious failures honestly, but he believes his motives are largely pure. As he looks around, he too sees a tragic world, but he reacts very differently. He believes all war, poverty, injustice, and oppression can be cured and we needn't wait for any plan of God to play itself out. Because his hope is for a more heavenly Earth, his primary struggle is to overcome what he perceives as the ignorance and selfishness of others. He views government as a savior of sorts, the best mechanism for engaging the ignorant and selfish to participate in his plan to reshape the world. What is needed is a hero—one who rejects the fatalism of the Fall; one with a vision for a new and better world. All that is needed is to gather together all those with good intentions. Together, they can make a more perfect world, and government is the logical vehicle for doing so.

The Fall and the Utopian Urge

Either man in the above example may have a perfectly reasonable desire to use government to help minimize the suffering and injustice brought about by the Fall. But if our understanding of the Fall is incomplete, then we may identify the wrong sources of that suffering and injustice, and we may be tempted to believe government can reverse the effects of the Fall. We may be tempted to believe that if government can simply get all of mankind pulling in the same direction, then war, poverty, suffering, and even death might be eradicated once and for all. If the Fall is not as complete as presented in the Bible, then Eden is within our grasp, and all men should stand ready to abandon their so-called "individual rights" if doing so will bring Eden one step closer for all men. If the Fall is not complete, then mankind can save himself, and government is the logical savior, and all men who stand in the way are selfish and evil by definition.

However, if the Fall is as complete as presented in the Bible, then Eden is not within our grasp, and government cannot bring salvation. Rather, government is a temporary and necessary evil. It may be employed to slow the downward spiral of mankind's depravity, and mercifully to blunt the full effects of the Fall, but government is powerless to reverse it. In fact, government should be approached with great caution. For if all of mankind is sinful, then government is sinful, too, which is of special significance because government possesses the power of coercion. Most importantly, we must be very reluctant to hand over whatever individual rights we have claim to, for government in a fallen world may well be on a fool's errand to do that which cannot be done.

In summary, the root of sin is the distortion of God's words, and one of sin's primary effects is the rebellious belief that mankind can recreate a better world than God has created—a humanistic utopia. If mankind doesn't like God's law as presented in the Bible, he can simply ignore it. Or he can rewrite it to suit his heart's desires. If he doesn't like the fact that God has defined *life* as beginning in the womb, then he can redefine life however he wishes. If he doesn't like the fact that God has defined *marriage* as between one man and one woman, he can recreate marriage to be whatever he wants it to be. And so on.

The errant view of the Fall is not restricted to one political party or another. Conservatives and liberals alike, even Christian conservatives and liberals, have in recent decades succumbed to the idea that government can be used to renew or transform our communities and to remake society. This is the Christian version of the utopian vision, also born from an incomplete understanding of the Fall, and it can lead to idolatry of government power. It can also lead to the tragic misallocation of Church resources, time, and energy.

The tragedy of Christian utopianism will be discussed in more detail in Chapter 9. For now, suffice it to say that, for the Christian, there can be no vision of utopia. Government in a fallen world is to be viewed as a necessary evil. It must be handled with great care, and its powers must be carefully limited. A complete and orthodox view of the Fall is the essential starting point. Only once the full depth and breadth of the Fall is comprehended can one begin to think biblically about the proper role of government. It is this truth—this biblical truth—that provides the basis for the doctrines of limited government and the separation of powers.

ENDNOTES

1   Genesis 2:16-17

2   Genesis 3:1

3   Genesis 3:3

4   Genesis 3:4-5

5   Genesis 3:7

6   In this section and the next, the author relies heavily on the teachings of R.C. Sproul in a recorded lecture series, entitled "Church and State," published by Ligonier Ministries, Copyright 1999.

7   Genesis 3:22-24

8   The exact power and function of the tree of life is not easily discerned. For our purposes, it is sufficient to note that God wanted to block Adam and Eve's access to it.

9   Romans 5:12-14

10 The Westminster Confession of Faith was written by an ecumenical gathering of English clergymen and laymen in 1646. It is a short but thorough summary of Biblical doctrine as understood by the most learned leaders of the Christian Church at the time, and is still used and admired today for its doctrinal clarity.

11 Charles Hodge, Systematic Theology, Abridge Edition, Edited by Edward N. Gross, P&R Publishing, 1988, p. 291.

12 Genesis 4

13 Genesis 6:5

14 Jeremiah 17:9

15 Psalm 51:5

16 Hodge, p. 301.

17 Romans 1:18

18 Romans 1:19-22

19 Romans 1:21-23

20 Romans 1:24, 26, 28

21 See Romans 1:22; Ephesians 4:17, 18; John 8:43; Matthew 13:14.

22 Ezekiel 11:19

23 Romans 3:10-12, citing Psalm 14:1-3, 53:1-3

24 See James 4:4.

25 Hodge, p. 298.

26 See Romans 2:14-16, 8:8.

27 Genesis 3:17-19

28 Ecclesiastes 2:23

29 Ecclesiastes 1:2

30 Romans 8:21-22

31 2 Peter 3:7

32 See Ephesians 2:1, 5; Colossians 2:13; Luke 15:24.

33 Genesis 3:19

34 Dorothy L. Sayers, Creed or Chaos, Sophia Institute Press, New Hampshire 1949, p. 45.

CHAPTER 4

The Separation of Church and State

Some may assume that Thomas Jefferson, Alexander Hamilton, or some other Enlightenment era political figure invented the idea of the "separation of Church and state." Others may think it started when Jesus Christ told the Pharisees to render unto Caesar that which is Caesar's, and render unto God that which is God's. But the concept of the separation of Church and state is older than the Federalist Papers and the Declaration of Independence. It is older even than the New Testament. It appears as a thread running through Scripture from the first few times God spoke to Moses in the Book of Exodus.

A Divine Division of Labor

Around 1400 B.C., the rulers of Egypt enslaved the nation of Israel (established by God through the line of Abraham). God sought to free them from bondage some 400 years later, and He selected Moses to confront Pharaoh, the king of Egypt, and lead the Israelites out of slavery and into the land of Canaan. Moses had been raised and educated in the Pharaoh's palace, even though he was a Jew. No doubt sophisticated in many respects, Moses feared that he lacked the eloquence to lead the people of Israel. He aired his insecurities before God, who begrudgingly appointed Moses' brother, Aaron, as an assistant to speak for him.[1] Gradually it became clear that Moses and Aaron were to play different but complimentary roles in the leadership of Israel. Moses was the most prominent public leader of the people. He contended with Pharaoh on their behalf (though it appears Aaron did most of the public speaking for Moses). Once the Israelites were freed, Moses led them through the desert and organized them into tribes. He even acted as a judge to resolve ordinary disputes among the people. All of this was done at God's instruction, and nothing could be clearer from Scripture than that Moses was a prophet of God who was in constant, daily fellowship with Him. The Psalmist even calls Moses a priest, because like Aaron, he was of the tribe of Levi, which was to be the priestly tribe.

Yet it was Aaron, not Moses, to whom God assigned the ceremonial role as Israel's first priest. Aaron would carry the rod through which God performed the famous miracles that helped convince Pharaoh to set the Israelites free. After the exodus, when God established a formal priesthood in Israel, Aaron and his sons were specially anointed for priestly duties.[2] It would be Aaron, not Moses, who would pass into the holy inner chambers of the sanctuary once per year to offer atonement for the sins of the people. And for the rest of biblical history, Jewish priests would be known as the sons of Aaron.

There is no doubt that during Israel's delicate infancy, it was essentially a theocracy. Even though Moses and Aaron played different roles, God ruled the nation of Israel. He spoke most often and most directly to His great prophet, Moses, who sought to carry out His will for the people. Yet there were already hints that the roles of civil leadership and the priesthood were best separated.

This feint theme appears again when the people of Israel clamored for a warrior-king to protect them from their enemies.[3] Although God warned Israel of the consequences, He eventually granted their wish, and selected Saul to be Israel's first human king. He ruled Israel from 971 B.C. to 931 B.C. From this point forward, the separation of Church and state becomes a discernable biblical pattern. Just as Moses had Aaron, the various kings of Israel always had the sons of Aaron, the priestly tribe of Levi, to perform the requisite priestly duties. So, from the very beginning, when God himself appointed the rulers overtly and structured the leadership of the nation He founded to accomplish his plan of salvation, He carefully divided the office of the king and the office of the priest.

During the reign of King Uzziah in the mid 700s B.C., we see another example. An otherwise great and beloved king of Judah (the southern kingdom of Israel, after Israel was split into two realms), Uzziah became very strong and prideful. On one occasion he entered the temple and shoved aside the priests so that he could perform the priestly ceremony of burning incense on the altar. By doing so, he sought spiritual authority in addition to his civil authority. Because Uzziah persisted despite grave warnings from the priests, God struck Uzziah on the spot with leprosy, and he later died in shame and misery.[4] Thus, even in this nation created and set apart by God to reflect His glory and bring forth the Savior, we see the origins of the separation of Church and state. If theocracy was inappropriate for this special nation, how much less appropriate would it be for other nations?

This pattern continues in the New Testament. A large portion of the New Testament consists of advice and counsel to the new Christian Church, complete with requirements for Church leadership. Yet there is no hint of a role for the Church in civil affairs. Although very few passages in the New Testament speak plainly on the matter, the very absence of Christ's attention to government—even the bloated, heavy-handed, pagan government of Rome—affirms the Old Testament separation.

Since the Enlightenment, theologically liberal scholars have argued that Jesus was primarily a political figure concerned with overthrowing unjust Roman rule. They read political activism into the life of Jesus, focusing on His ethical teachings to avoid His controversial claims to deity. But the accounts of Jesus' life contain little in the way of political activism. There is no question that Jesus deplored the injustice of the oppressive Roman rule over the Israelites. But there is also no question that Jesus' ministry was not focused on fixing the government, or on a political revolution of any kind. His attention was directed at the salvation of individual human beings, regardless of their earthy circumstances. Nothing could be clearer from Scripture: Christ was not crucified as punishment for political activism of any sort. He was crucified for His claims to be the divine Messiah.

THE SEPARATION OF CHURCH AND STATE

The clear separation of Church and state throughout biblical history was not lost on the early Church, or on the Church through the ages. In the chapter on civil government in the *Westminster Confession (1646)*, we read the authors' doctrinal conclusion, that "God, the Supreme Lord and King of all the world, hath ordained civil magistrates to be under him over the people, for his own glory and the public good.... The civil magistrate may not assume to himself the administration of the Word and sacraments, or the power of the keys to the kingdom of heaven...."

It is important to note that not only is the separation of Church and state rooted in the Bible, its origins can be traced nowhere else in history or literature. It is a uniquely biblical concept. Keeping in mind the biblical truth that God has established all authorities, including the Church and the state, we can depict the biblical view of government simply:

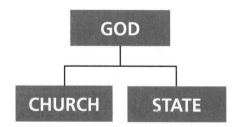

The Power of the Sword

The Apostle Paul tells us that it is the civil government, not the Church, to which God has given the power of the sword[5] (meaning the authority to use force). As you will recall from Chapter 3, this authority is the essential aspect of government. It encompasses the use of force domestically to coerce and to punish, and to wage war with other nations who might threaten the citizenry. Nowhere in Scripture is the Christian Church given this power.

But what if a government is composed of Christians who think God wants them to destroy an unbelieving nation? May they use the power of the sword for such a purpose? Wouldn't this be consistent with the wars fought by ancient Israel at God's direction? In Old Testament times, God did at times instruct the people of Israel to make war. God instructed Joshua, Moses' successor, to lead the people into many battles and to claim the land of Canaan for Israel. These battles were brutal, and God sometimes instructed the Israelites to set mercy aside and kill even women and children.[6] In fact, God revealed himself to Israel as a warrior fighting on the side of His people.[7] Moses once described the God he knew so well as a "consuming fire."[8]

This is a difficult truth for Christians, but one we cannot ignore. Why would God call for the use of force to such a degree? Here are two feasible explanations. First, prior to the advent of Christ and the age of the Church, God used Israel as an instrument of judgment on other nations to shame and discredit their idols and to reveal them as false and futile.[9] In the case of Canaan, God used Israel to judge a people who had adopted a culture so sinful it is difficult for us to imagine.[10] As one example of their depravity, the Canaanites had adopted the regular practice of ceremonially sacrificing children to idols.[11] The same God who previously ordered the destruction of almost all of mankind via the great flood[12] likewise used Israel to bring judgment upon the people of Canaan. Second, God used warfare to establish the nation of Israel amidst a hostile, fallen world, to usher into the world His only Son, our Savior, Jesus Christ.

Whatever the reasons, however, the wars fought by Israel at God's direction took place in a unique time in biblical history. The Bible simply cannot be used honestly to justify a holy war today. Now that Christ has come bearing the Gospel of salvation by grace, God's people are no longer identified with any one nation. The new people of God—the true children of Abraham—are those who confess their sins, repent, and believe that Jesus Christ died on the Cross to save them and then rose from the dead to lead them.[13] Under this new covenant of grace, the people of God are scattered throughout all nations, tribes, and races. There is therefore no scenario under which it would make sense for God to again use a particular nation to fight wars in His name.

This is not because God has changed or softened His judgment after Old Testament times. Not at all. He is still the God of judgment. But He is also the God of mercy. By His mercy, God—even right now—is forestalling judgment during the age of the Church, the age of Gospel evangelism. He truly desires that none should perish. But we must remember that God will again send His Son in the flesh to bring judgment on the Earth. And the One who saves also will judge. Bone chilling accounts of judgment day can be found in the Book of Revelation and elsewhere in Scripture. But because God desires that none should perish, He has tasked His Church with preaching the Gospel until that day arrives.

While God in His mysterious but sovereign ways may still use warfare among nations to accomplish various purposes in this fallen world, our ability to discern those purposes is extremely limited. But one thing is beyond debate: The Gospel of Christ is never to be spread by warfare, violence, or coercion of any kind, but only by the power of the Holy Spirit.

Given this framework, tragic seasons in the history of the Church (such as the Crusades, the Spanish Inquisition, and the Salem witch trials) come into clearer focus. These episodes, regardless of the motives behind them, were the unfortunate results of religious authorities, or government authorities, or both, exceeding their biblical authority. Although sometimes violent campaigns have been carried out in the name of God, His name was being used in vain, and biblical support cannot be found for such endeavors.

The Sword of the Spirit

The Church is, of course, the Body of Christ on Earth. It is the visible gathering of those who have put their trust and faith in Jesus Christ as their Lord and Savior. As such, God has assigned the Church very different responsibilities than those He has assigned to civil government. God has given the leaders of the Church, referred to in the Bible as "bishops" or "elders," what Jesus called the "keys to the kingdom" of God.[14] Keys are a sign and symbol of authority. So when Jesus entrusts the keys to the kingdom to Church elders, this means that the elders of the Church act as gatekeepers of a sort with respect to who enters the visible Church and who does not. The Church is also tasked with administering the sacraments of Baptism and Communion (also called "the Lord's Supper"), and some Christian traditions recognize other sacraments that are similar in nature to these. Regardless, the duty to administer the sacraments is assigned to the Church and to the Church alone. Last but certainly not least, the Church is tasked with the ministry of the Word of God. This entails the teaching and preaching of the Bible, as well as the shepherding of the flock toward biblical obedience.

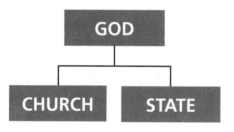

CHURCH	STATE
Keys to the Kingdom	No Keys
No Sword	Power of the Sword
Ministry of the Word	No Ministry of the Word
Sacraments	No Sacraments
Baptism	
Lord's Supper	

It is critically important to understand the biblical division of labor between Church and state. We might summarize the division by saying that the Church is tasked with matters of the soul, and the state is tasked with matters of civil conduct. The Church operates in the realm of the human heart—the inward man. The state operates in the realm of civil society—the outward man. The Church wields the sword of the Spirit, the Word of God, to accomplish its purposes. The state wields the sword of physical force to achieve its responsibilities. The Church's prime directive is to lead man to peace with God. The state's prime directive is to keep the peace among fallen men. The Church's authority extends only to members of the Church. The state has responsibility for all citizens.

The Temptation of Theocracy

Although the Bible teaches that God has assigned very different roles to Church and state, both remain under the authority of God. God is the creator of all things, including government, and His Word is the only source of final authority. This is a difficult concept to grasp, especially in a world in which many people, in fact most people, are not Christians and do not recognize the Bible as their authority. The most common error that religions and religious people (even Christians) sometimes make with respect to the roles of Church and state is to completely merge the two. This is a move toward theocracy, which is an un-biblical view of government.

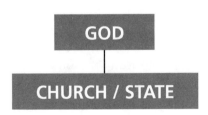

Theocracy views the state as a primary vehicle through which God works to accomplish His spiritual purposes for all people. One example of a religion that embraces theocracy is Islam. Americans sometimes have difficulty grasping the nature and goals of Islam because they tend to view it as just another of the world's religions, like Buddhism or Hinduism. But Islam is more than a religion. As noted earlier, it includes a system of government in which the religious law, called "sharia," becomes the law of the land for all citizens. It is therefore a civil structure as well as a religious one, and its goal is not only to foster belief in Allah, but also to enforce religious behavior, using the power of the sword, on all peoples of all nations and all religions. The mosque possesses the power of the sword—the power to use force—to enforce the teachings of Allah. In fact, the very symbol of Islam is the sword, and Islamic history is a chronicle of religious warfare.

The conflation of Church and state can be a temptation even for Christians, whose doctrine doesn't support it. Christians have committed this error at various times throughout history. Constantine declared Rome a "Christian Empire" in 312 A.D., entangling the Church in civil governance. The Roman Catholic Church wielded the power of the sword during the Crusades in the Middle Ages, to defend the Holy Land from Muslim invaders. Though undertaken as defensive measures, the Crusades resulted in atrocities committed under the sign of the Cross and in the name of God.

Unlike Islam, which comingles the duties of Church and state, this error is an especially tragic one for Christians, because it is anathema to the Gospel. At the heart of the

Gospel of Jesus Christ is the teaching that sin cannot be cured by outward behavior. Sin can be overcome only by the power of God working from the inside out—when the Holy Spirit applies the death and resurrection of Christ to the human heart. In other words, the Gospel knows nothing of the use of government authority to compel Christian behavior or to coerce or destroy unbelievers.

But what about voting for laws that force people to behave morally for the good of society? As we will discuss in more detail in Chapter 9, Christians have a duty to stand for laws and policies that reflect the truth, and to stand against those that represent falsehoods. But if the temptation becomes to use the government as a substitute for the Holy Spirit to force people to show respect for God, or even to pray or attend church, this is not the biblical role of the state; and as history has shown, it is a most regrettable error. The Bible teaches that government, like all earthly institutions, was created by God and is accountable to Him, but because He has carefully defined the roles of Church and state, there can be no biblical Christian theocracy among men.

ENDNOTES

1   Exodus 4:10-17

2   Exodus 28:1; Lev. 8:1; Leviticus 4:3

3   1 Samuel 8

4   2 Chronicles 26:16-23

5   See Romans 13, especially verse 4.

6 See, e.g., Deuteronomy 2:34-35, 3:6-6; Joshua 11:19-20; Jeremiah 19:5, 32:35.

7 See, e.g., Deuteronomy 3:22; cf. Jeremiah 21:5, where God actually fights against His own people, the people of Judah (in the southern kingdom of Israel).

8 Deuteronomy 4:24

9 Jeremiah 11:11-12

10 Joshua 11:19-20

11 Deuteronomy 12:31; Jeremiah 7:31

12 Genesis 6:5-7

13 See, e.g., Romans 4:13-25.

14 Matthew 16:19

★ CHAPTER 5 ★

Divine Limits on Government Authority

So far we have learned that God established the authorities of Church and state and gave them different roles. God, as the Creator, remains in authority over them. Yet we have also learned that God's authority over the state is not intended to result in a theocracy. How, then, is civil government to behave? If civil government is under God's authority, and yet is not tasked with enforcing or spreading Christianity, what exactly is the relationship between God and government?

In Chapter 3, we learned that the purpose of government is to make and enforce laws that restrain evil. This protects mankind from the full effects of his own rebellion and lawlessness—the effects of the Fall. But we have also learned that government is not the Church's enforcer. The government has no power, authority, or ability to judge human hearts or to change them. Its role rests primarily in the arena of controlling outward behavior to keep civil order. Some laws, such as laws governing traffic in the streets, present almost no dilemma. They clearly fall within the purview of civil government and are fairly easy to define. Not every duty of government is so easy to identify.

Because the purpose of government is to restrain evil, rulers must often make judgments about what is good and what is evil. When government ventures outside the narrow realm of physical protection and the basic maintenance of civil order, stark moral judgments must be made. In making moral judgments, the government should be constrained by the truth of God. It has no authority to overrule Him. In this chapter, we will explore the limits of government authority in making moral judgments. Using examples from God's moral laws (those that are particularly applicable to keeping public order), we will see how God constrains government and rules over it without resorting to theocracy.

The Moral Law Constrains Government Power

After God used Moses and Aaron to free the Israelites from bondage in Egypt, God began to prepare the Israelites to be His people. He gave them detailed instructions on how they should live and worship. The books of the Bible immediately following Genesis (Exodus, Numbers, Leviticus, and Deuteronomy) contain the many laws and rules given by God to His people. Chief among them were a set of moral laws that we call the Ten Commandments:

You shall have no other gods before me.

You shall not make for yourself a carved image, or any likeness of anything that is in heaven above, or that is in the earth beneath, or that is in the water under the earth. You shall not bow down to them or serve them....

You shall not take the name of the LORD your God in vain....

Remember the Sabbath day, to keep it holy.

Honor your father and your mother....

You shall not murder.

You shall not commit adultery.

You shall not steal.

You shall not bear false witness against your neighbor.

You shall not covet your neighbor's house; you shall not covet your neighbor's wife, or his male servant, or his female servant, or his ox, or his donkey, or anything that is your neighbor's.[1]

Unlike the Old Testament ceremonial laws and the many civil laws God gave specifically to the nation of Israel, God's moral laws are universal and eternal. The ceremonial laws presented in the Old Testament were fulfilled in Jesus Christ's life, death on the Cross, and resurrection. The purposes of the civil laws—to establish the nation of Israel from which the Savior would come— have been accomplished.[2] But the moral law stands forever, and is unchanging. It places duties on every human being whether they know it or not, and whether they recognize

God's authority or not. This is true of politicians, judges, and citizens alike.

Using the Ten Commandments as an example of God's moral law, we can see that the first four commands are fundamentally spiritual commands. They reflect duties owed by all people directly to God. Under the gospel of grace, obedience to these commands must originate in the heart. The mere outward performance of those duties is meaningless to God. So governmental authority—the power to force compliance with laws—has no clear role to play.

The remaining six commandments pertain to duties owed by each man to his fellow man. Some of these six apply directly to our conduct in civil society. Under the gospel of grace, authentic obedience to these commands must originate in the heart as well. However, because some of these commands relate to man's treatment of his fellowman, obedience to these laws can foster societal order and civil peace. Here, there is a role for government enforcement of man's outward behavior.

For example, consider the commandments "You shall not commit murder" and "You shall not steal." From these two commandments we learn some very important information about God's design for human government. As with all of God's laws, there is more to these commandments than meets the eye.

The Basic Duty to Safeguard Innocent Human Life

By issuing the command against murder, God reveals to us that human life is precious to Him. Later, in the Book of

Matthew, Jesus expounds upon the deeper meaning of this law. He says if we harbor hatred in our hearts for another person, we have broken this commandment. This is because hatred causes us to objectify the person we hate. When we objectify another person, we put ourselves in the seat of the judge, and we in effect reject him as a creature of God. By failing to show the person compassion, forgiveness, or love, we also reject the compassion, forgiveness, and love that God may be extending him. All murder stems from this mindset, so hatred is equal to murder in God's eyes. The command "you shall not commit murder," then, places very personal duties on the individual person. We are not to hate people and we are not to objectify people. We can address these matters of the heart effectively only by applying the truth of God as found in His Word. This is the proper rule of the Church.

When a hate-filled heart leads to outward behavior such as violence or murder, however, the government has an important role to play. It must use its authority to curtail violence and punish murder. This government role seems fairly obvious, but the command "you shall not commit murder" carries a deeper implication as well. Murder is the taking of innocent life—but who gets to define what constitutes *life*? Because God issued the command in the first place, His interpretation of it should control. Because government authorities are responsible to God for enforcing this command, He will hold them responsible if they ignore His clear guidance on what it means.

Some have argued that the command, "You shall not murder," and its attendant charge to protect human life forbid capital punishment and war. They believe that because God treasures human life, there is no circumstance under which one man has authority to take the life of another. This is not, however, the biblical view. We know the command, "You shall not murder," does not forbid the government from capital punishment or warfare for several reasons. First, the Hebrew word for "murder" does not encompass killing in the context of a just punishment by a proper authority, or killing in a just war. It refers to the taking of innocent life or to the taking of life without authority.

Additionally, the Ten Commandments were delivered by God to Moses alongside many other laws. Among them were laws governing the proper application of capital punishment and laws governing warfare. Reading the command in context, then, it is obvious that the prohibition against murder did not preclude capital punishment or war. Of course, by placing strict guidelines around capital punishment and warfare, God confirms the high value He places on human life.

Therefore, capital punishment and warfare should be conducted only with the most careful and reverent concern for justice. Authorities must proceed with great caution in those areas because the improper application of force can indeed result in murder. But because capital punishment and warfare are sometimes necessary for the protection and preservation of innocent human life, God has authorized the use of deadly force by civil authorities, and He will hold them responsible for its proper use.

From this commandment, Christian scholars have long derived one of the primary responsibilities of government:

To protect, support, and maintain innocent human life. Sometimes, in a fallen world, this requires government to use deadly force in the form of capital punishment or even warfare. The protection of innocent human life is perhaps the first and most fundamental duty of government as delegated by God to the civil authorities. But while this commandment empowers government in some ways, it constrains government in at least one important respect—government is not free to create its own definition of life. It is constrained in its duty by God's definition—because God issued the command in the first place.

The Basic Duty to Safeguard Private Property

Similarly, in the command "You shall not steal," God is telling us that the idea of personal property is not a man-made idea. It is His idea. For if He did not intend for humans to own property, there could be nothing to "steal," and thus no need for this commandment. God knows that owning personal property is part of what it means to be a human being, and He strictly forbids the taking of property from others without permission. Of course, stealing is not merely breaking and entering someone's house. There are countless ways in which we might take things—both tangible and intangible—from others. We steal by checking the wrong box on our tax returns, by not returning something that was borrowed, by using our time at work for personal purposes, by taking credit for something we did not do, or by taking less than honest measures to win a promotion at work. The command, "You shall not steal," tells us that God hates stealing. It is a matter of His justice. When a person works to obtain a possession, or otherwise comes by it fairly, no one should take it from him.

Like murder, theft begins in the heart. There is nothing government can do to change the sinful state of the human heart. Again, this is the business of the Church. But government can use its authority to punish and deter theft to promote civil order and peace among citizens. The command "You shall not steal" has deeper implications for government, however. Because the commandment reveals that God values personal property, government must not simply deter and punish the physical act of stealing, it should *honor* personal property as God honors it.

Personal property is important to God because to deprive people of their personal property is to enslave them. A man works for his wages and uses his wages to acquire property for the benefit of himself and his loved ones. His possessions, therefore, represent the fruits of his labor. When someone takes them from him, he has nothing to show for his labor. He has, in effect, worked for nothing. This is why it is a fundamental responsibility of government to protect the personal property of citizens (which entails, among other things, the regulation of agreements between men, the upholding of contracts and the enforcement of standard weights and measures in commerce). It is also why rulers should use the power to tax with restraint, as a tax is merely a means of appropriating the fruits of a man's labor.

From this commandment, then, Christian scholars have derived another primary responsibility of government: To protect personal property. But while this commandment empowers government in some ways, it also places an important constraint on government, because it reveals that God places a high priority on the right of the individual to enjoy the fruits of his labor. A man's property—and his ability to earn wages to acquire that property—are precious to God. Because God charges government with enforcing this moral law, it must also accept God's interpretation of it. Government that properly serves under God's authority will not claim the power to redefine the value of the individual nor the value of the individual's God-given right to enjoy the fruits of his own labor.

There are other commands in Scripture that could be applied to government. For example, God's command to Adam to "subdue the earth" implies a duty of environmental responsibility and stewardship. But as we search for the very fundamental responsibilities of government, these two emerge as most easily identifiable: To protect, support, and maintain human life, as God defines life; and to protect the dignity of the individual, which entails the respect and protection of his personal property.

Many other religions and man-made ethical systems contain prohibitions against murder and theft. An argument can be made that the Bible is not unique in that respect. But there is no other religion or man-made system that presents this simple yet sublime structure for a government and a Church, existing side by side, each with its own role, each constrained by and accountable to God for the proper execution of its duties. This framework is the only known haven between theocracy and tyranny. It is the only framework for a society that can be free yet pluralistic, and it is found only in the Bible—it comes from the mind of God:

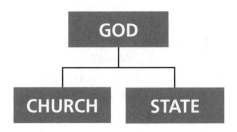

CHURCH	STATE
Keys to the Kingdom	No Keys
No Sword	Power of the Sword
Ministry of the Word	No Ministry of the Word
Sacraments	No Sacraments
Baptism	Protect Innocent Life
Lord's Supper	Protect Personal Property

Sadly, even though this framework is the only path to a lasting, free, and pluralistic society, mankind simply will not abide a societal structure in which the government is accountable to the God of the Bible. Ever since the Fall, mankind has fought to free himself from the authority of God. Believing he could make a better world if he rejects God's authority over government, he has done just that. He has established government as a free-floating authority that is no longer accountable to God and no longer constrained by God's revealed truth. In the next chapter, we will see how the Western world has replaced the biblical view of government with a thoroughly secular view—and then we will see the results.

ENDNOTES

1 Exodus 20:3-17; See also Deuteronomy 5:7-21.

2 The civil laws given by God to Israel were applicable to Old Testament Israel and are not binding on other nations in other times. They are, however, still useful guides. For example, Charles Colson, in his writings on the death penalty, pulls principles from the civil laws given by God to Israel to analyze the laws governing capital punishment today. He notes that Israel's laws did not allow for restitution in cases of murder; and that they required a high standard of evidence to convict a man of a capital crime. Mr. Colson argues that we can learn from these biblical principles in our application of capital punishment today. See Charles Colson, "Capital Punishment: A Personal Statement," http://www.freerepublic.com/focus/f-religion/1274579/posts, November 8, 2004.

PART III

Government's Revolt Against the Authority of God

THEY EXCHANGED THE TRUTH ABOUT GOD
FOR A LIE AND WORSHIPED AND SERVED THE
CREATURE RATHER THAN THE CREATOR.

ROMANS 1:25

★ CHAPTER 6 ★

New Roles for Church and State

Under the biblical view of the separation of Church and state, the two institutions play distinct roles in society, but both are under the authority of God. The state is not to operate as a theocracy, but it should be viewed—and should view itself—as a steward that must answer to God and draw on His revealed truth to govern justly. Yet, when mankind fell into sin, he rejected the authority of God and is now seeking to build his own kingdom of heaven, under his own authority, on Earth. Saint Augustine viewed human history as an epic struggle between the City of God and the City of Man. Marx, Engels, and Stalin saw history in much the same way, though they were rooting for the other side. Certainly, being a sinner does not mean a man is destined to be like Joseph Stalin, nor that he will cause government to kill, steal from, or oppress his fellow man. But it does mean that all people and all governments naturally rebel against the notion that God stands in a position of authority over them.

The roots of this rebellion against the authority of God are found in the Garden of Eden, as we have seen. It can be traced through subsequent human history by following the materialist philosophers Epicurus and Lucretius in ancient times, to modern atheist philosophers such as Jeremy Bentham, John Stuart Mill, Karl Marx, and John Dewey (to name a few). Between them, these men and others succeeded in convincing much of Western society that good and evil are not determined by God, but by man. Thus, it would be foolish to allow any of the various religions or their various moral laws to have any influence on the affairs of state.

The modern Western view of a totally secularized state is the legacy of Marxism. Marxism has proven itself a failure, even a disaster, but the West remains enamored with Marx's call for an entirely secular state. It is also the legacy of the French Revolution. Just after the American Revolution was fought and won to establish a complimentary separation of Church and state, the French Revolution was fought and won to establish a "conflictual" one.[1] Largely due to these influences, the prevailing view today is that God may have established the Church, and He may have authority over Church affairs, but He did not establish the state and has no direct authority over it. Thus God—if He exists at all—governs only in the realm of personal preference, which is entirely separate from the realities of life that concern the state and over which the state has supreme authority.

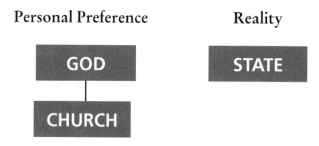

This is how the West's secular worldview distorts the traditional and biblical doctrine of the separation of Church and state. Under this secular view, the state is not answerable to any higher power for its actions. It is unrestrained. The state has total, autonomous authority over the lives and affairs of men in civil society. God is left to govern only matters of the heart, all of which are reduced to personal preferences and sentiments. When John F. Kennedy said in his historic 1960 speech, "I believe in an America in which the separation of Church and state is absolute," he was defending his Catholic faith. But in doing so, he gave voice to the increasingly popular view that the separation of Church and state is something much more than a division of labor.

The U.S. Supreme Court Leads the Way

When one uses terms such as "rebellion" and "revolt," pictures come to mind of bloody coups, with wild-eyed, blood-thirsty masses storming the capital. While mankind's revolt against the authority of God has been a remarkably bloody affair,[2] it has been relatively subtle in some corners of the Western world, particularly in America. If there is any doubt in your mind that such a rebellion has taken place in America, however, that doubt will be satisfied simply by reviewing a few Supreme Court cases.

The rebellion became easily visible in a 1971 case called *Lemon v. Kurtzman,* a case involving government aid to private schools. In that case, the Court handed down what has become known appropriately as the "Lemon test." From that point forward, other federal courts would use the Lemon test to determine if a law violates the First Amendment's prohibition against the establishment of religion. To pass First Amendment muster after *Lemon,* the state must show that the law in question (a) has a secular legislative purpose, (b) will have a primary effect that neither advances nor inhibits religion, and (c) does not foster an excessive entanglement with religion.

The first part of the Lemon test was the most significant, because if the state could not articulate a secular purpose for a law, it would be struck down, regardless of how the rest of the Lemon test was applied. At first glance, the Lemon test does not seem entirely unreasonable. After all, the United States is not a theocracy, and most people would agree that the law should not be used to further purely religious ends. Although the lower courts struggled to apply the Lemon test consistently, few laws were struck down, because most courts interpreted the first part of the Lemon test as blocking only those laws that were passed by legislators solely for the purpose of advancing religion. In other words, only purely religious laws—laws that had no secular purpose at all—would be struck down under the Lemon test.

But the Court took things a step further in a 1987 decision entitled *Edwards v. Aguillard*. In *Edwards*, the Court reviewed a Louisiana law requiring that evolution be taught as a theory (not as fact) in public schools, and that creation theory be given equal consideration in classrooms. The state of Louisiana argued that their new law had several secular purposes—to teach evolution more accurately, to allow additional scientific facts into the classroom (which had previously been excluded in textbooks and by teachers), and to promote the academic freedom of teachers in public schools. The *Edwards* court applied the Lemon test and struck down the Louisiana law. In doing so, the Court reinterpreted the first part of the Lemon test. Previously, the Court struck down laws under *Lemon* only if those laws had no secular purpose. But in *Edwards*, the Court struck down the Louisiana law because the Court believed the law was *motivated* by religious beliefs. The legislative history behind the Louisiana law clearly showed that the law would accomplish the secular purposes mentioned above. Until *Edwards*, this was all that was required to satisfy the Lemon test. But because the *Edwards* Court deduced that the lawmakers who voted for the law did so out of religious motives, it struck down the law, and thereby banned numerous scientific facts from the classroom merely because they coincide with certain religious beliefs. After *Edwards*, the Court would no longer base its Establishment Clause decisions on the *purpose* of the law, but on the *motives* of the legislators. So even if the law has a properly secular purpose, it can still be struck down if the Court determines the legislature was motivated, even in part, by a religious belief.

In essence, *Edwards* banned religious belief from the legislative chamber. The Supreme Court of the United States made formal the pattern that had been developing in America for some time: that of a complete separation between Church and state. And because, as Yale professor Stephen Carter observes, "by some estimates, an absolute majority of the law now on the books were motivated, at least in part, by religiously based moral judgment," [3] the stage was set for a wholesale restructuring of the American legal system. America had taken the West's revolt against God to another level.

The idea that the law should be morally neutral thus became the law of the land. It quickly became a matter of legal and philosophical sophistication to establish one's own personal *wall of separation* by drawing a line between one's personal beliefs and one's public policy positions. This gave rise to the nonsensical statements (discussed in Chapter 1) such as, "I personally believe that abortion is wrong, but I do not believe my personal beliefs should be the law of the land," and "I personally believe that marriage is between one man and one woman, but I do not believe my personal beliefs should be written into the law for everyone." As discussed earlier, these types of statements represent a belief that one's views about God and morality are merely personal preferences that cannot and should not have any bearing on one's policy positions.

But because all laws contain a moral imperative of some kind, the Supreme Court has very difficult work to do. Detecting religious motives can be difficult. The Court has made its work easier, however, by refusing to define exactly what is meant by a religious motive. As long as it refrains from defining its terms, then it is free to make whatever determinations it wishes. For example, if a law is passed that bans all abortions, then because the pro-life movement is aligned with Christian belief, the Supreme Court might simply find that the legislature was unduly motivated by religious purposes and overrule the ban. Conversely, laws motivated by other worldviews, such as secular humanism (which declared itself a religious movement in *A Humanist Manifesto* of 1933), might be upheld by the Supreme Court, simply because the Supreme Court has not clearly defined its categories. This allows the Court to rule however it wishes on a given law, giving the First Amendment's Establishment Clause a very different effect than was originally intended. It was originally intended to allow religious belief to flourish in America by forbidding the federal government from enforcing one particular state religion, but it has become the means by which the government enforces strict compliance with the religion of secular humanism. Ironically, while the biblical view of Church and state rejects theocracy, this distorted *wall of separation* results in something almost indistinguishable from a secular humanist theocracy. Author and commentator Mark Levin observes:

> The American courts sit today as supreme secular councils, which, like Islam's supreme religious councils, dictate all manner of approved behavior respecting religion. Whereas the supreme religious councils enforce Islamic law, the supreme secular councils have seized for themselves the mission of segregating God and religion from public life and have immersed themselves in religious matters. Neither of the councils tolerates

conflicting or diverse viewpoints, insisting that their rulings are the final word for all society.[4]

Government Without God

Here is the danger in the prevailing secular view that entirely severs the two spheres of God and government: when God is completely removed from government, our inalienable rights become alienable. Under the prevailing secular view, we cannot make reference to God's moral law. We cannot even acknowledge that our rights come from God, because that is too religious a statement. But if our rights are not granted or defined by God, they must be man-made. They must be granted by the government alone. If they come from the government, then they are completely subject to the political process. They are subject to change. Mere *wants* and *desires* can now become *rights* if it is politically expedient to so elevate them.

Americans have become all too comfortable with the idea of appealing to the government to declare our *desires* to be *rights*. When we claim a *right* to view pornography, that homosexuals have a *right* to marry, or that a woman has a *right* to have an abortion, what we really mean is that we desire these things desperately, and we are begging our new god—the government—to elevate our desires to the status of moral law. The state thus goes from being the guardian of eternal, unalienable, rights, to the all-powerful creator, definer, and grantor of rights. Under this secular view of government, the government can ration or even reverse rights that once were held *unalienable*. The state giveth, and the state taketh away.

The government, then, has rejected its role as the protector of our God-given rights, and has claimed the authority to grant, withhold, and redefine those rights. This has given new intensity to interest-group politics, as everyone scrambles to join voting blocs powerful enough to pressure the government to grant or protect their particular desire. If all rights are up for grabs, those with the most political power will win. No one's rights are sacred anymore.

When the Various Views Clash in the Public Square

The various views of Church and state are a source of friction in America today. One very large and growing group of Americans holds the prevailing secular view. They believe that our fundamental rights are merely ideas written on paper that are subject to change with the next Supreme Court decision, or the next vote in Congress. Another group holds to a more biblical view, believing that our fundamental rights come from God and should therefore be recognized, affirmed, and protected by government, but cannot be changed by government. This second group used to reflect the vast majority but now seems to be declining in numbers and influence. Some religious sects believe that the Church and state should operate as a theocracy. Although these people are very few in number and carry no influence in Western society, the fear of theocracy is palpable to those who hold the secular view.

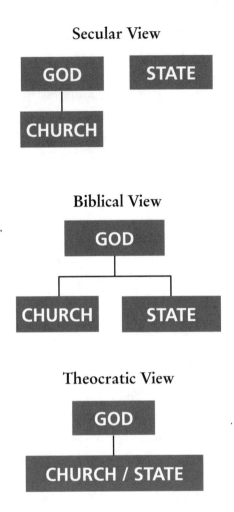

The clash between the various views is on frequent display in American public life. Periodically a liberal-minded politician will make a strong statement about his or her Christian faith, and there is no outcry from the media. But when a more conservative-minded politician makes a statement regarding his or her Christianity, suspicion and anxiety arise. Consider that in the 2008 Presidential campaign, the Republican and Democratic nominees were openly Christian, as were both of their Vice Presidential running mates. Barak Obama, Joe Biden, John McCain, and Sarah Palin all professed a healthy Christian faith. But it was only the faith of Sarah Palin, a conservative Christian, that caused public concern. Of the four, hers was the only faith that could be characterized as "evangelical," meaning she likely held the Biblical View. But the secular world does not understand biblical teachings, and so a concern that she might hold the Theocratic View gave rise to countless news segments and articles about the potential dangers of Sara Palin obtaining high office. The other candidates were all presumed to hold the Secular View, which poses no problem in the eyes of the secular media. They were exempt from suspicion and free to speak about their faith as they wished with little or no criticism.

The clash between views is never as evident, though, as during Senate confirmation hearings for Supreme Court Justices. These hearings can become very contentious and frustrating for everyone involved, primarily because vastly different views of the separation of Church and state are being voiced at the same time. Many of the people on the Senate panel, whether Democrats, Republicans, or Independents, hold the Secular View. If the judge leans toward the traditional conservative viewpoint, and especially if he or she is a Christian, he will likely hold the Biblical View. This makes it very difficult to communicate.

On September 14, 2005, at the Senate confirmation hearings for Justice John Roberts, Senator Dianne Feinstein (D-Calif.), asked Judge Roberts (later confirmed to the Supreme Court, now the Chief Justice) whether he believed in the separation of Church and state as set forth in the First Amendment. She quoted President John F. Kennedy as having said in 1960, "I believe in an America where the separation of Church and state is absolute." Feinstein added, "My question is: Do *you*?"

Judge Roberts answered, "Senator, I think the reason we have the two clauses in the Constitution in the First Amendment reflects the framers' experience. Many of them or their immediate ancestors were fleeing religious persecution. They were fleeing established churches. And it makes perfect sense to put those two provisions together: no establishment of religion and guaranteeing free exercise. That reflected the framers' experience."

Feinstein responded, "You can't answer my question yes or no?"

Judge Roberts replied, "Well, I don't know what you mean by absolute separation of Church and state."

Most often, the majority of the Senate panel wants the judge to say that he will not allow any religious views to influence rulings. While the judge may understand the question, it is a difficult one to answer. If the judge holds the Biblical View, then he believes there are separate roles for Church and state; but the judge cannot possibly say what the Senate panel wants to hear—that he will leave behind all of his religious views about the nature of truth, the nature of reality, the nature of man, our duty to obey the law, and the origins of our fundamental rights. When he struggles to make a clear statement that the Senate panel requires, some on the panel may begin to suspect he holds the Theocratic View. They become concerned the judge may secretly harbor plans to institute a religious theocracy, in which he can use his newfound authority to bring Church authority to bear in the public square.

This dynamic is also at work when the religious faith of the judge is made known. When President George W. Bush appointed Justice John Roberts, who was presumed to be a moderate conservative, he and his wife were subjects of suspicion for their devout Christian beliefs. Later, when President Bush appointed Sam Alito, who was known to be a conservative, there was great concern because he would be the fifth Catholic on the Supreme Court, giving Catholic Christians a majority of seats on the Court. But in 2009, when President Barak Obama appointed Justice Sonya Sotomayor, also a Catholic Christian, but known to hold a more liberal political position, there was no public concern about her religious faith whatsoever.

One might think this would be the other way around. Roberts and Alito, being relatively conservative in their judicial philosophies, generally do not believe that a judge should allow his personal sympathies to drive a personal agenda in judging. However, Judge Sotomayor, prior to her confirmation hearings, publicly stated that her personal background and sympathies were an important influence on her decisions from the bench. Why were the Senate and media so much more concerned about the Christian faiths of Roberts and Alito than Sotomayor? It is because the world knows that a liberal-minded Christian likely holds the Secular View, and because the world fears that more conservative minded Christians hold the Theocratic View. Because the world does not understand the Biblical View, they do not know how to distinguish between it and the Theocratic View, and therefore cannot always properly evaluate the judges' responses. While it can be entertaining to watch this dynamic at work in the public square, it actually marks an important step in the decline of America, and in Western civilization. By accepting the absolute separation of Church and state, we have lost the ability to think rationally about the origin of fundamental human rights.

But Isn't a Secular Government Necessary in a Pluralistic Society?

Still, one may fairly ask, "How can non-Christians be expected to live under a government that is organized using biblical principles? Do all citizens need to become Christians?" Indeed, it might seem egocentric for Christians to believe that their God, and no one else's, should be the God of government. There is, however, a very practical response to this question: Christianity is the only religion—the only worldview—that accounts for the existence of basic God-given rights for the individual while also allowing for the separation of Church and state. It is also the only worldview that allows for a truly pluralistic society. The Christian view of government not only allows for citizens to be non-Christians, it assumes that most citizens will fall into this category. Because Christianity calls for a reasonable separation of Church and state, people of all faiths, or of no faith, can live peacefully under the Christian structure. Using a biblical metaphor, you might say that the Christian model for government creates a tree in which all kinds of birds might nest and find food and refuge.[5] This is not true of any other religion or worldview. As discussed in Chapter 1, the Christian worldview is entirely unique and particularly suited to freedom and pluralism. Even when fully adopted, the Christian view of government will not result in a panacea. In our fallen world, even a properly organized government is subject to corruption, immorality, and rebellion. There is no doubt that the Biblical View has been abused and distorted in the past. But a proper understanding of it remains the only hope.

The Biblical View is the only model that encourages limited government, and thus freedom, in a pluralistic society. The Secular View of government—widely believed the best model—cannot long sustain a free and pluralistic society. It cannot produce a free society because it recognizes no limits on governmental authority. Government will inevitably increase its own authority at the expense of freedom. There is nothing to constrain it from delving into all aspects of life to *fix* what is wrong. Nothing prevents it from redefining the value of life—even life itself. It cannot produce a tolerant society, because it actually fosters intolerance. True diversity springs from a diversity of ideas—of beliefs. But under the Secular View, all religious belief systems are treated as equally irrelevant to matters of public policy, and are relegated entirely to the private sphere. Those who do not conform to the secular belief system become outsiders, even threats.

In contrast, under the Biblical View, rulers must view themselves as stewards of the authority entrusted to them by God. They do not personally possess power. Instead, they are in a position of trust and of service to the creator and giver of all life and all rights. Under the Biblical View, leaders do not have to be Christians, but they must fear God and realize that they are under-servants to Him.

> Now therefore, O kings, be wise; be warned, O rulers of the earth. Serve the LORD with fear, and rejoice with trembling. Kiss the Son, lest he be angry, and you perish in the way, for his wrath is quickly kindled. Blessed are all who take refuge in him.[6]

Why should non-Christians ever agree to live under the biblical model for government? Because a lasting free society must be built upon this biblical model; if it is built on any other, it will not last, or it will not be free.

ENDNOTES

1   *Without Roots*, p. 110 (drawing from the Pope's thoughts).

2   By far, most of the suffering of the nations in the 20th century was foisted upon people by their own misguided and power hungry governments, in the form of ill conceived wars, pogroms, purges, and cleansings, and often as a result of their own utopian visions. See Niall Ferguson, *The War of the World: Twentieth Century Conflict and the Descent of the West*, The Penguin Press, New York, New York, 2006. Stalin, Hitler, Mussolini, and Hirohito all took part in purges and wars designed to implement their vision of a perfect society.

3   Stephen Carter, p. 111.

4   Mark R. Levin, *Liberty and Tyranny*, Simon & Schuster, New York: 2009, p. 33.

5   In both the Old Testament and the New Testament,
    comparisons are made between a good kingdom and a tree
    in which the birds of air built their nests. In all instances, the
    "birds of the air" represent Gentiles—unbelievers—who seek
    rest and refuge in the kingdom of the Messiah. *See* Matthew
    13:32, Ezekiel 17:23, Daniel 4:12.

6   Psalm 2:10-12

★ CHAPTER 7 ★

A New View of the Individual

Believing itself freed from God's authority and all biblical constraints, government quickly moved to redefine key truths of God. Where to start? Actually, for secular government to establish itself firmly as the highest authority in the land, the starting place is obvious. *It must redefine the individual.* If God creates individuals in His own image, as the Bible teaches, then individual people are infinitely valuable to God, and government would be constrained by some pre-defined responsibilities. It would be duty bound to protect human life (as defined by life's Creator), and to preserve their property and individual rights. Under the weight of these burdens, government's ability to reinvent society would be seriously hindered. For the newly secularized government to consolidate its power and achieve its vision, the idea of the individual must be redefined. The Western idea of *individualism* must be discredited, along with its biblical roots.

Individualism and the West

One of the great pillars of Western culture is Individualism. Individualism is the idea that the *self* is a unique and distinct being—a free moral agent, bearing the personal responsibilities of self-control and self-improvement. It encompasses the idea that each human being, individually, is possessed of an immortal soul of infinite value. It recognizes that man will rise and fall in both material wealth and worldly power, but nothing that is obtained or achieved in this life can increase or decrease the essential value of the individual person.

This conviction of the high value of individuals is such an integral part of Western culture that most Westerners would not recognize their culture without it. It is hard to imagine that individualism does not exist in all cultures, but it doesn't. It is a uniquely Western idea, and is perhaps the most significant and distinctive aspect of Western culture. It is certainly the aspect of Western culture most hated by our enemies (think of the Communists and the Radical Islamists).

Individualism gives rise to the notion of equality before the law. This is the idea that every law should apply in the same way to each individual citizen, regardless of his religion or race, wealth or poverty, or his station in life. Individualism also spawned the right to vote—democracy itself—because it demands that each person's opinion is valuable, and that no one should deign to rule others by force or oppression. Indeed, individualism is the fuel for freedom itself. Each man is a responsible moral agent, and no other man should dictate the course of his life or determine his destiny for him.

Of course, this aspect of Western culture comes with a price, but Americans and other free peoples historically have accepted it. The price of equality before the law is that sometimes, when you believe you deserve special treatment, you will not get it. The price of democracy is that sometimes your preferred candidate will not win or your preferred law will not pass. And the price of freedom is that no one can guarantee how well you will fair in the vast societal competition. And yet, for at least a few hundred years, Westerners and particularly Americans have boldly made the bargain, judging equality, democracy, and freedom well worth the price.

Individualism and Christianity

Today, it is a common belief among Westerners that all people are essentially equal and should be treated with equal dignity and respect. It is, however, a vaguely held belief. Most people on the street do not know from where it comes. Of course, the ideas appear in the founding documents of the United States, but if that is where they originated, we are all in trouble. Documents can be reinterpreted, amended, or changed.

Individualism did not arise from the dust of the ground. It is not the product of evolution or rationalism. While we find shadows of it in early Greek philosophy, in the semi-free economic structure of medieval European city states, and in Renaissance thought, individualism in its fullness is a concept found exclusively in the Bible. It is a Judeo-Christian idea, born from the revelation that God made man in His image. According to secular British researchers Richard Koch and Chris Smith, with the rise of Christianity:

[T]he idea of individuality was emphasized in a new way, linked both to God, and to a moral imperative to improve oneself. Individuality meant development—and obligation, fostered by awareness of God's amazing, unlimited love, to become a better and more useful person. It is difficult for us today to grasp quite what a breathtaking, what an astonishing and counter-intuitive worldview, this notion of personal and individual potential and obligations was at the time. It started with the totally original Christian claim that the all-powerful God, maker of heaven and earth, was deeply interested in the well being of every individual person in the world. "God so loved the world, that he sent his only Son" to earth, to suffer and save not humankind at a collective level, but individual humans. Salvation operated at the level of the single person. For the first time ever, Christians believed in a personal God, able to relate to separate humans. The Christian God had a direct and deep interest in human matters, and an urgent interest in every human being, whatever their status or nationality. To Greeks or Romans, the concept that God—any god—cared about individuals, still less about what they did, was simply unbelievable. Even many early Christians, especially if they were not Jewish, found this belief difficult to swallow. Yet the mainstream Christian view of responsibility before God prevailed, transforming the course of Western history.[1]

The Old Testament prophets preached not just to the priests, but also to the people. They individualized morality, and treated each listener as a responsible moral agent before God. Later, Jesus Christ would go further. In the Book of John we read that Christ said, "If anyone loves me, he will keep my word, and my Father will love him, and we will come to him and make our home with him."[2] When Christ said this, and other things like it, He was saying things no one had ever said or thought before. Second only to the Gospel itself, it was probably the most radical and wonderful thing that had ever been said. Each person, as an individual created by God, has the capacity to have direct fellowship with Him. It was a statement that would change the world.

Among other things, it would destroy the idea that a person was born to be a mere integer in the larger equation of humanity; no person was born inferior to another in the thing that mattered most. It would shake the previously unchallenged foundations of oppression, slavery, castes, and the divine right of kings. It would put a stake in the ground, once and forever, reminding all peoples of all nations that a person—an individual—is never a means to an end. In the eyes of God, the individual himself is an end.

It is the Bible alone that tells us of a God who is personal, who creates each individual with a plan and for a purpose, and who speaks to him. It is the Bible that tells us of a God who loves people enough to send His only Son to die on a Cross. But that death was not undertaken for humanity as a race; it was much more personal than that. Christ died on the Cross for individual persons. If we accept His sacrifice for our sin, He will save us from our destiny of eternal punishment in hell, and usher us into eternal life with Him in Heaven. The glory of the

Cross is that this salvation is available to anyone who trusts in Christ and follows Him. It is available to the worst sinner and the most persnickety do-gooder. It is available to people of any race or religion. It is available to the rich and the poor, and to those of high station and low. He knew you before you were born. He knows your thoughts and your heart's desires. He knows every hair on your head. When you kneel before Him and submit to His Lordship, you become his adopted son or daughter. And when you die and go to Heaven, you will remain yourself in all essential respects. In summary, God created you, He knows you, He has spoken to you, and He will save you if you are His. Until Jesus said it, the world had never before heard anything like it, and no one who hears it can ever be the same afterwards. God's plan, as mysterious as it is, focuses on individual people: you and me.

This biblical individualism is inherent in Christ's admonition to "love your neighbor as yourself." This commandment, which Christ calls one of the greatest commandments of all, is predicated on the idea that our neighbor—whether rich or poor, powerful or weak, believer or unbeliever—is worth loving. He is worth loving because God loves him. God's love for individual people gives them inherent worth, and places on all of God's children a duty to love others as He does. This is the very foundation of a free and civil society. There is no other.

Westerners have become so conversant in the language of Individualism, it is tempting to believe it is mankind's natural state. But nothing could be further from the truth. As the Bible teaches, men are naturally inclined to seek refuge within the larger group. That is why Christ refers to people as sheep. We find comfort being one of many, a mere face in the crowd. We are like Adam and Eve, who desired to hide from God in the bushes. We want to blend into the mass of humanity in hopes that He will not find us. We will do almost anything to avoid personal accountability to God. Just as the ancient Jews believed they were saved by being a member of the Jewish community, many of us seek refuge in our affiliations. But Christ calls us out one by one. He calls us out of hiding and demands that we commune with Him as individuals. He tells us that one day each of us must stand before the throne of God and give an account of our life. In other words, individualism is not a self-indulgent doctrine leading to anarchy, it is a call to stand up and recognize one's own accountability before God. It is a command to apprehend the dignity of being a child of God.

Indeed, Christianity cannot be properly understood apart from individualism. The idea that God deals with people on an individual basis is at the heart of the Gospel. He can save a person from any nation, and of any affiliation or background. You are not beholden to or restricted by a priest who stands between you and Christ. Instead, the Bible teaches of "Christ in you,"[3] and initiates a priesthood of all believers. When Martin Luther stood alone against the errant institution of the Catholic Church, sparking the Reformation, he was merely expressing the most fundamental aspect of biblical faith—that through Christ, he had his own relationship with God, and that his own trust in Christ would save him.

The idea that God loves and deals primarily with the individual is the basis of individualism, and individualism is the foundation of freedom. Not only does it provide the individual accountability and self-governance that freedom requires, it furnishes the only reasonable basis upon which a thinking man would accept the risk of being free. Freedom entails competition. Free people compete for resources and benefits in nearly everything they do. In education, business, and politics, nearly everything amounts to a competition of sorts. This adds an element of risk to nearly everything we do, because in a free society in which everyone is equal under the law, there are no guarantees of success. Given the dangers of this world and the unpredictability of life, why would anyone choose to be free? Why would anyone want to live in a society that does not promise protection against the risks of living in this dangerous world? A reasonable man would choose to live in a free society only if he held some very particular beliefs: that God knows him personally, understands his plight, and controls his ultimate destiny, which is separate and apart from the perils and injustice of this world.

To summarize, Western individualism is founded upon the biblical teaching that each person is created by a personal God, and in the image of God. Individualism is the idea that each individual in society has inherent dignity and value—it is the essential ingredient to freedom. You will not find this same idea in other religions. In most other religions, God is either impersonal or indifferent to man. You certainly will not find any basis for the value of individuals in atheism or agnosticism. In fact, there is no basis for such a belief apart from the teachings of Christianity. The entire free world has borrowed the idea from the Bible.

Exchanging Individualism for Collectivism

And yet, Individualism has come under heavy attack in the West, even in America. Westerners no longer know the meaning of the term, and have converted it into a pejorative word to describe the selfish, materialistic, side of modern Western culture. It marks someone who is prideful and careless about the consequences of his actions on the world around him. Individualism is viewed today as being responsible for the breakdown of society and the fracturing of communities.

Although individualism arises from fundamental biblical truths, and has provided the very foundations of freedom, it is now decidedly out of fashion. "Collectivism," the old enemy of individualism, has taken its place. "Community" is now the darling of Americans, secular and religious alike.

Here we reach a very important distinction. Collectivism is a secular idea that is the opposite of individualism. Collectivism is the idea that people gain their identity, their worth, and even their value from the community of which they are a member, and not from God. The collectivist looks over society and doesn't see individuals, but people groups. His goal is not to protect and uphold the individual, but to protect and uphold *communities*. Although God established the idea of private property for individuals, the collectivist believes private property is the cause of human suffering and inequality. He therefore believes that communities, not individuals, should own private property. At its very worst, collectivism holds that truth itself is not entirely objective, but is found only in what works for, and what is embraced by, a particular community.

While those who espouse individualism tend to believe that the law should treat individuals equally, regardless of the circumstances, the collectivist believes something very different. He believes the law should be a tool for leveling out people's circumstances within the entire community. In doing so, he must treat individuals unequally under the law, and thus he subjects the value and dignity of the individual to the needs of the broader community. Collectivists are often very compassionate and loving people who believe that what is best for the community is best for the individuals who reside in that community. But by placing a higher value on the community and a lesser value on the individual, the collectivist does something very dangerous, and in most cases, very unbiblical. He reduces the individual to a mere integer in a larger equation. The individual becomes expendable in pursuit of a supposedly greater purpose. The individual becomes a means to an end. This is the first step towards tyranny.

The word *tyranny* may raise eyebrows because many people associate it with militaristic dictators who wear strange uniforms and give angry speeches at staged rallies, or with pogroms and political prisons. When we think of a tyrannical society, we think of tanks rolling through the streets and people huddled in dark basements to evade the secret police. This type of militarism, however, is not the essence of tyranny. The essence of tyranny is the subjugation of the individual to a broader vision of a new society. Once a government subjugates the dignity, importance, and value of the individual to its vision of the "good of the community," then freedom is hindered and tyranny is born.

Tyranny and the Good of the Community

Tyranny often descends upon society not with machine guns and secret police (though these are the favorite tools of many tyrants), but with a phalanx of mundane regulations. Over-regulation of the individual's existence reduces the individual to a lifeless animal of the state, forced to live beneath the weight of someone else's notion of a *better society*.

Imagine a working man who lives in the suburbs. A company offers him a promotion that would require him to commute across town, but a government regulation caps his daily auto emissions. He cannot afford a new car with a cleaner engine, so he is unable to make the commute. He must decline the promotion. He dreams of opening his own business at home and wants to turn his garage into an office, but the extra living space would result in a higher property tax, and state and federal employment laws make it too costly to hire helpers, so he cannot afford to pursue his dream.

To obtain a business loan, he has to prove that he possesses health insurance that meets government standards; but he currently carries a lower cost plan that doesn't meet the standard. He bought the lower cost plan to save money to send his daughter to nursing school. To enroll, she was required, under a new regulation, to show proof of her own health insurance. After paying for additional insurance, his daughter had to seek partial government funding for nursing school, but to pay it back, she must volunteer at a government clinic that performs abortions.

He is glad to have free public schooling for his younger son, but he cannot be as involved in his boy's education as he would like, because to promote racial diversity the public school bus transports the boy to a school that is an hour away. The school teaches a full sexual education curriculum in the third grade, which equates heterosexual sex with homosexual activity, and traditional marriage with gay marriage. His son learns very little about the American Constitution or its framers, but he knows all about the radical environmental agenda, Vietnam, and Watergate. He has learned to be suspicious of the American military and all forms of religious fundamentalism; and he has learned that Franklin Delano Roosevelt was the greatest American president in history.

These are the beginnings of a soft tyranny. Alexis De Tocqueville put it this way:

> After having thus successively taken each member of the community in its powerful grasp, and fashioned him at will, the supreme power then extends its arm over the whole community. It covers the surface of society with a network of small, complicated rules, minute and uniform, through which the most original minds and energetic characters cannot penetrate, to rise above the crowd. The will of man is not shattered, but softened, bent, and guided; men are seldom forced by it to act, but they are constantly restrained from acting; such a power does not destroy, but it prevents existence; it does not tyrannize, but it compresses, enervates, extinguishes, and stupefies a people, till each nation is reduced to be nothing

better than a flock of timid and industrious animals, of which the government is the shepherd.[4]

This is tyranny that comes in the form of smiling, affable, educators, and politicians who speak in lofty tones. "It would be like the authority of a parent, if, like that authority, the purpose was to prepare men for manhood; but it seeks, to the contrary to keep them in perpetual childhood."[5] Because collectivism results in weaker, more dependent individuals, it weakens society overall. But the collectivist is not deterred. They strive to persuade others that the foundations of Western civilization are not all they are cracked up to be, and that life will be better if they turn from their individualistic (read "selfish") ways and allow the government to improve life for everyone.

The movement to nationalize the American healthcare system presents a fascinating example of how collectivism ultimately results in the diminishing of individual rights and freedom. Twice in the last twenty years, there has been a focused effort by American politicians to nationalize the American healthcare system. The nationalization of healthcare presents a classic example of a soft tyranny, because it requires the forced exchange of one's individual rights for a vague promise of a better society for all. On June 24, 2009, newly elected President Barak Obama appeared on an ABC television news program to discuss his plans to take steps toward nationalizing the American healthcare system. During a question and answer session, a woman named Jane Sturm asked the President a fascinating question:

My mother is now over 105. But at 100, the doctors said to her, "I can't do anything more unless you have a pacemaker." I said, "Go for it." She said, "Go for it." But the specialist said, "No, she's too old." But when the other specialist saw her and saw her joy of life, he said, "I'm going for it." That was over five years ago. My question to you is: Outside the medical criteria for prolonging life for somebody who is elderly, is there any consideration that can be given for a certain spirit, a certain joy of living, a quality of life, or is it just a medical cutoff at a certain age?

This is a fascinating question because Ms. Sturm and her family, having recently been through a very delicate and personal healthcare decision, were curious to know if a national system would be capable of recognizing the nuances of their particular situation. On paper, it was no doubt a risky expenditure of resources to obtain a pacemaker for a 100 year-old woman. And yet, living in a free society as they do, they apparently found a willing doctor and committed to spend much time and no doubt personal resources to obtain the pacemaker. It turned out to be a wise decision. Now hear President Obama's response:

I don't think that we can make judgments based on people's *spirit*. Uh, that would be, uh, a pretty subjective decision to be making. I think we have to have rules that, uh, say that, uh, we are going to provide good quality care for all people. End-of-life care is one of the most difficult sets of decisions that we're going to have to make.

But understand that those decisions are already being made in one way or another. If they're not being made under Medicare and Medicaid, they're being made by private insurers. At least we can let doctors know—and your mom know—that you know what, maybe this isn't going to help. Maybe you're better off, uhh, not having the surgery, but, uhh, taking the painkiller.

Although President Obama may be a warm, caring, person in his own right, he could not have demonstrated more clearly the cold, cruel, and unfeeling nature of a government that views its individual citizens as expendable—as means to larger ends. President Obama is no doubt sincere in his desire to see a net improvement in healthcare across all of the healthcare statistics to which he has access. But Ms. Sturms' mother is not a statistic. She is a human being. She is a mother. She is a person. She is a child of God, created by God. She and her family enjoyed the freedom to make a very difficult decision. Their doctor did, too. No doubt all of them considered the risks, the costs, and the potential benefits. Ultimately, they evaluated her *spirit* and zeal for life, and their personal decision resulted in five more years of life, and counting.

But President Obama struggled with Ms. Sturms' question because as compassionate a man as he is, he is not focused on individuals. His worldview requires that he not think of Ms. Sturms' mother as a person, but as an integer in a larger equation. In this equation, the better course of action may have been to consult a set of government standards and give Ms. Sturms' mother "the painkiller" instead of the pacemaker, which would allow the government to ration one more pacemaker to someone younger. Ms. Sturms' mother would likely be dead. But to those who support government-controlled healthcare—so long as the government's rules regarding pacemakers require us to deprive all 100 year-old people of life-saving operations—we will have equal healthcare for all. They would take the Sturms' decision out of the hands of the individual and give it to government policy makers who have never met or even seen Ms. Sturms' mother. Is this what the Founders meant when they spoke of "equality?"

Tanks or no tanks, this is tyranny: when one person or a group of people elevates their vision of a *better society* above the dignity and worth of the individual. When this happens, those in power view all of mankind as a single instrument. The individual becomes insignificant, and whatever helps to "usher in the final state of happiness" becomes the new secular moral imperative.[6] Anyone who opposes the vision is by definition *evil*.

Many Americans gasp at the thought that the Communist government of The People's Republic of China imposes a one-child policy on its citizens. In many cases, couples who have more than one child are forced to abort their additional children. The leaders of the Communist party in China did not, however, show up for work one day and decide that millions of babies should be aborted for no reason. No doubt they engaged in a seemingly rational analysis to address important societal issues: overpopulation, poverty, dwindling resources, harm to the environment, etc. Yet their policy—while no doubt designed to benefit society as a whole—has led to a barbaric law that calls for millions of individual people to be put to death. Americans do not believe anything like this could happen to them. History, and the Fall of Man, portend otherwise.

Consider another example from a hypothetical courtroom on a typical day in America. Before the judge stand a wealthy man, a middle-class man, and a poor man. Each has committed the same crime, which normally brings a one-year prison sentence. If the jury determines that each of the men actually committed the crime, the judge's role is to treat them equally before the law.

But what if the judge believes his role is to do more? What if he believes his role is to engineer outcomes that, in his opinion, encourage the evolution and improvement of the larger society? The judge may know the rich man, and believes him to be an otherwise good man who donates money to local charities and whose business employs many people in the community. The judge believes that, although the rich man has broken the law, the community will be harmed if the rich man is incarcerated, so he waives the lawful sentence and sets the man free.

Similarly, looking at the poor man, the judge feels sorrow for him and decides to show him mercy. He believes the community will be harmed if the poor man is released destitute onto the streets in one year. If he is set free now, with a stern admonition from the bench, he can continue to work and the society at large will not have to support him. So the judge waives the lawful sentence for the poor man, too.

The middle-class man, however, is one of many middle-class men in society. He is of no special value to society like the rich man, and his temporary incarceration would pose no societal financial strain. So the judge determines the middle-class man must face *justice*, and sentences him to the full one-year jail term. By the end of the day, the judge may feel as if he has used sound judgment and appropriate mercy in delivering justice. But he has done no such thing. In fact he has undermined the principle of equality before the law, and with it, the very foundations of freedom.

By allowing his personal judgments of what is best for society to override his legal duty, the judge has invited politics into his courtroom. The next time someone is accused of a crime, his lawyer will know the law is not the final word. If he can appeal to the judge's political sensitivities, he might spring his client even though he is guilty. Do you see what has happened? Now the judge, not the law, stands as the sole deciding authority. The rules of justice have become subjective and malleable. Punishments are now discussed and decided not on the basis of the law, which is supposed to be the same for everyone, but on the basis of the judge's personal vision for a better society. The individual's personal responsibility has become less important than the judge's social agenda. The person standing before the judge is seen not as an individual who is guilty or innocent, who must be held accountable for his actions, but as an integer in a larger equation of the judge's own political calculation. Now those who appear before the judge have an incentive to identify themselves with the various groups or causes that the judge prefers. Of course, if you are successful in identifying yourself with a preferred group, you will be treated with mercy. If you are not, you will be treated harshly. Once the interpretation of the law becomes a political tool, no two people are truly equal before the law, and tyranny wins another small victory.

You may ask, "Where is there room for mercy and wisdom in your description of equality before the law? Shouldn't Christians, above all, use discretion and show mercy to those in need? Shouldn't we at least desire mercy for the poor man?" These are fair questions. Of course Christians should be people of mercy. But these questions beg more questions. Is the judge actually showing mercy? Is it the judge's role to rewrite the law and impose his own vision onto society? And is it truly merciful for a judge to place the good of society over the dignity of the individual?

The judge is supposed to be a steward with a particular charge: to uphold the law. If the judge does not uphold the law, but instead overrules the law in accordance with his personal preferences, this is not mercy. Although the word *mercy* can be used to provide cover, the judge is usurping the power of the people, and setting himself up as a mini-tyrant. If he wants to show mercy, he may do so personally by visiting them in prison, assisting their families while they are gone, or helping them get reestablished when their sentence is complete. But it is not mercy to show favoritism to the rich man. Nor is it mercy to rob the poor man of his dignity by implying that he is too pitiful to be held responsible for his actions. To punish him less is to say to him, "We do not expect as much from you as a rich man." President George W. Bush called this misguided mercy "the soft bigotry of low expectations." The judge is not showing mercy at all. He is robbing people of their dignity as individuals.

True equality before the law is a precious thing. In order to secure it, Americans have historically been willing to trade vastly unequal circumstances. They have done so because they know, if given enough political and economic freedom, individuals can change their circumstances for the better. But once the government claims for itself the power to equalize the circumstances of the people in its charge, freedom is in danger, and equality before the law will become a thing of the past.

ENDNOTES

1 Richard Koch and Chris Smith, *Suicide of the West*, Continuum Publishing Company, London 2006, pp. 36-37.

2 John 14:23

3 Colossians 1:27

4 Alexis De Tocqueville, *Democracy in America*, edited and abridged by Richard D. Heffner, Penguin Books, New York 1956, pp. 303-304.

5 Alexis De Tocqueville, *Democracy in America*, edited and abridged by Richard D. Heffner, Penguin Books, New York 1956, pp. 303.

6 *Roots*, p. 72-73.

CHAPTER 8

New Definitions for Life and Marriage

Once secular government supplants individualism with collectivism, the struggle against God's authority becomes progressively easier. If society no longer views government as answerable to God, and no longer views the individual as a child of God, then the *good of the community* becomes the imperative. And because the categories of *good* and *evil* have been detached from truth, *good* and *evil* become a matter of opinion. They can be changed through the political process. The two most prominent and divisive examples of this are the movements for abortion rights, and the rights of gays to be married.

Government Declares the Unborn to Be *Unpersons*

As discussed in Chapter 5, one of the most essential duties of government is to protect the lives of the people under its charge. In the case of unborn human life, many Western nations have abandoned this duty. Everyone acknowledges government's duty to protect life, but God's definition of *life* has been rejected, and the new secular definition excludes the unborn. In America alone, since *Roe vs. Wade*, over forty-million unborn children have been aborted—killed in the womb or just outside the womb—with the blessing of the government authorities.

Much has been written on the scurrilous origins of the abortion movement in America, which has always been more about racism, eugenics, and radical environmentalism (population control) than about women's rights. Much has also been written about the effects on a society that allows the extermination of forty million of its own population: a diminished tax base to support an aging population, a labor shortage leading to uncontrolled immigration, and a shrinking military.

For the Christian, however, the primary reason to oppose abortion is that it is unbiblical. Long before the science of genetics confirmed that a fetus is a human being, the inspired authors of the Bible knew it was true. The Bible teaches us that God forms each human being in the womb and that He knew us by name even before the foundation of the Earth. In the Book of John, when we read that the unborn John the Baptist was filled with the Holy Spirit, we know intuitively that unborn children are truly people: because God doesn't send His Holy Spirit into any other type of earthly being. Thousands of years before, when God gave the civil laws to the nation of Israel, His law treated an unborn child as a human being. God's definition of human *life* includes the unborn.

In truth, everyone knows that *life* includes the unborn and that abortion is wrong. Any mother who has had an abortion knows it by her personal pain. Even the most vocal pro-choice advocate doesn't defend abortion on the merits. Instead, he characterizes abortion as an issue of women's rights. Just as any good Southern slave owner would rather defend slavery using the language of state's rights to avoid the horror of the behavior they were defending, so every good pro-choicer can opine eloquently about women's rights to avoid the horror of the behavior they are defending. Just as for the slave owner, the plight of the slave was not considered; so for the pro-choicer, the plight of the unborn is a non-issue. Politicians in particular will almost never speak positively of abortion. As discussed earlier, they prefer statements like, "I personally believe it is wrong, but ..." So Christians are not alone in their conclusion that abortion is wrong. The difference is whether the government should support it or ban it—and remember, the government cannot be neutral on the issue because no law is neutral.

The case that abortion is an offense to God is beyond question; and yet Christians often struggle to stand firmly against it. Why? Many Christians have fallen for the secular idea that abortion is a personal decision, and that Christians should keep their beliefs to themselves. We saw some of the flaws in that line of thinking earlier. But there is yet another reason why Christians have struggled to make the case against abortion.

Many people believe it is hypocritical to advocate less intrusive government while also promoting a legal ban on abortions. A legal ban is thought to require more powerful and more intrusive government. This charge of hypocrisy is often the rhetorical coup de grace in the debate over abortion. It has all but stymied pro-lifers. Al Gore used it in his first presidential debate against his opponent George W. Bush, and Bush quickly (and conspicuously) changed the focus of the discussion. If pro-lifers are looking to change the abortion laws by first changing the hearts and minds of pro-choice Americans, then they must learn to face the hypocrisy charge head-on and overcome it.

How then should a Christian view the government's role with respect to abortion? Is it reasonable to suggest that a government that outlaws abortion can be less powerful and less intrusive than one that permits them? Absolutely. Our government's failure or refusal to act is not always a sign of a less-powerful government. Government that has become too bloated and powerful might also fail or refuse to intervene on behalf of particular citizens, just as a decadent, self-indulgent monarch might yawn and roll his eyes in response to a peasant's plea for justice. One of our federal government's most fundamental roles is to protect the lives and liberties of its people. It does not possess the constitutional power to decide which groups of people it will and will not protect. It follows that when our government begins picking and choosing which people deserve protection, it is engaging in an arrogant power grab.

Our federal government appears to have taken a passive posture on abortion that favors the freedom of women to exercise *choice* in their private lives. On the surface, such a government may seem deferential and non-intrusive— the kind of government conservatives prefer. But the government only looks passive because it is delegating its authority. As discussed in Chapter 2, by permitting abortions, the government delegates to expectant mothers the power to strip an unborn human being of any and all rights, so that it can be put to death with no legal ramifications. *In other words, the government delegates to women the right to treat their unborn children as unpersons before the law.* Of course, before it can delegate a power, the government must first claim that power for itself. By claiming the power to declare certain persons to be *unpersons* and then delegating that power, our government is choosing to reject its constitutional obligation to protect the lives and liberties of a particular class of people. It has redefined *life* to exclude the unborn. This is hardly smaller government; it's a case of government power spinning out of control.

Our government's tolerance of abortion is reminiscent of our government's former tolerance of slavery. The government never required anyone to own slaves, nor to treat African-Americans as *unpersons*. Whether to enslave an African-American or treat him as an unperson was purely a matter of individual choice. By failing to ban slavery prior to the Civil War, leaving it as a matter of choice, the government essentially delegated to white people the power to treat African-Americans as unpersons by enslaving them. Today, Americans agree that a government possessing the power to declare African-Americans unpersons before the law is one whose power has reached dangerous proportions.

It follows, then, that a government that permits abortion—like a government that permits slavery—is far too powerful and intrusive. To pass a law, therefore, that requires the government to protect the unborn is to limit the government by restoring a sense of proportion to government power. Such a law would stand as a reminder that a legitimate government has no right to declare certain human beings less than human, or to refuse to guarantee their full human rights.

Of course, many pro-choice advocates would claim precisely that an unborn child is something less than a human being; and, indeed, if unborn children were truly not human, then it would be perfectly reasonable to declare them unpersons. Thus we have the strange marriage between the pro-choice movement and the scientific theory that "ontogeny recapitulates phylogeny." Also known simply as "recapitulation," this is the theory that a fetus passes through various stages (from protozoan to fish to frog to bird to primate and finally to human) while in the womb. This theory has been a great help to the pro-choice movement, because it makes an early-stage abortion akin to killing germs on a kitchen counter, or flushing a goldfish down a toilet. Clearly, if a fetus is nothing more than a germ or a goldfish, then it should not enjoy government protection at the expense of the mother's freedom. Such protection would constitute blatant discrimination against women.

Unfortunately for the pro-choice movement, the German scientist who originated the theory of recapitulation, Ernst Haeckel, fabricated his famous drawings of the fetus going through the various stages. Still, the theory is so valuable to proponents of macro-evolution—many of whom are, naturally, pro-choice—that many school textbooks still teach it as a scientific fact. To this day, many people who attend public grade school learn the theory without qualification, despite the fact that Dr. Haeckel's fabrications were exposed as far back as 1911!

Dr. Hymie Gordon, a physician and professor of medical genetics at the Mayo Clinic, points out that science has now progressed to the point that: "We can now say that the question of the beginning of life—when life begins—is no longer a question for theological or philosophical dispute. It is an established scientific fact. Theologians and philosophers may go on to debate the meaning of life or purpose of life, but it is an established fact that *all life, including human life, begins at the moment of conception.*"

It is understandable that Christians are sensitive to the charge of hypocrisy. But in the case of abortion, the charge is completely false. It is perfectly consistent to support smaller, limited, less powerful government, while at the same time demanding the government outlaw abortion. Ironically, it is indeed hypocritical when Christians vote for pro-choice candidates when the Bible so clearly teaches that abortion is wrong.

Should Christians be one-issue voters? Absolutely. There is nothing wrong with being a one-issue voter if the one issue is important enough. A Christian does not have to vote for someone who is pro-life just because the person is pro-life, but a Christian should never vote for a pro-choice candidate or support pro-choice laws. To do so is to give government powers that God never intended. The conscientious Christian has no choice but to take a stand against all forms of abortion. The most fundamental biblical role of government is to protect human life—as the Giver of life defines it. Secular society distinguishes between types of human life whenever it is convenient to do so. God does not; and therefore Christians should not.

Government Claims the Power to Redefine Marriage

In the case of abortion, very few people would say publicly that abortion is right. The issue of gay marriage is different. More and more people seem to believe that there is nothing wrong with gay marriage, and more and more people are willing to say so publicly. Still, gay activists tend to avoid arguing for gay marriage head on. Most often, they frame the issue in terms of discrimination. They make a convincing case that gay couples are the victims of religious bigotry, and that they want nothing more than to be set free from the moral shackles placed on them by others. To be a good American, they argue, one must set aside one's personal beliefs about gay marriage. We can already hear politicians saying, "Personally, I believe gay marriage is wrong, but I do not believe the laws of the land should deny gays the right to be married." (Sound familiar?)

The homosexual lobby claims to loathe moralizing, but underneath their talk about discrimination and intolerance is a profound and sweeping moral judgment: that there is nothing supernatural—nothing transcendent—about heterosexual marriage or sex, and so human government has the authority to redefine them at its whim. Essentially, their claim is that it is *immoral* for the government to refuse to recognize gay marriage. If the debate is to be properly joined, supporters of traditional marriage must insist that the gay activists defend the morality (or immorality) of their beliefs.

If the advocates of gay marriage are to make a valid case of discrimination, they have some further explaining to do. Discrimination is not inherently unjust. It is unjust only when we give unequal treatment to people or things that are essentially the same. So when someone cries discrimination because the law does not recognize gay marriage, what he is really saying is that homosexual sex and marriage are essentially the same as heterosexual sex and marriage. Before the law is changed to allow gay marriage, the gay activists (and the judges who seek to empower them) should be required to explain this essential similarity.

Some gay activists try to meet that burden by defining marriage as the legal recognition of a committed, loving, relationship between adults. But that is incorrect. Marriage is not, and has never been, the mere recognition of committed and loving relationships between adults. Many adults love one another and are committed to one another (a grandmother and her adult grandchild, or war buddies, or close sisters, and the like), but these commitments have never been considered marriage. No one would argue that these relationships are essentially the same as a heterosexual marital relationship. So it remains an open question why two homosexuals should qualify for marriage merely because they claim to love one another dearly.

Gay activists might also argue that marriage is the formal recognition of a monogamous sexual relationship, and since the Supreme Court recently removed all legal barriers to homosexual sex, the government should likewise bestow formal recognition on monogamous sexual relationships between homosexuals. But let us not forget that two homosexual people are anatomically incapable of having sex with one another. The mutual stimulation engaged in by homosexuals is very different from sex, for which heterosexual couples are uniquely equipped.

Given these differences, the burden lies squarely on the homosexual activists to press the case further. To do so, they must delve into religion and morality. If they want government to redefine sex and marriage, they must be required to explain the very origins of sex and marriage and prove that human government has the authority to redefine them. Therefore, they will have to argue, first, that heterosexual marriage is either merely a man-made social construct or else the result of blind social evolution; and second, that the sexual organs of males and females were not designed to fit together for any special purpose beyond mere biological reproduction.

Looking at the debate in this light, it becomes clear that gay activists are engaged in that which they purport to hate. They are trying to force their worldview (be it religious or irreligious) onto their fellow Americans. This is their prerogative, of course. It is the very purpose of legislatures to debate the rightness or wrongness (read *the morality*) of the law, and it is the very purpose of elections to try to force one's beliefs onto others by electing one's preferred candidate over the preferred candidate of one's neighbor.

Supporters of traditional marriage should not fear the struggle over the morality or immorality of gay marriage. Rather, they should fear that our lawmakers—or worse yet, our courts—might make a decision without addressing the real issues: Are we certain that there is nothing supernatural about heterosexual sex and marriage? And are we certain that human government should claim the authority to redefine them?

The strongest defenders of traditional marriage defend it because they believe God instituted it. They believe that government merely *recognizes* marriage, and cannot redefine something it did not create. The strategy of the gay activists is to remove marriage from this vaunted status and bring it down to Earth, where mankind can tinker with it. Their claim is that government—not God— has the sole authority to define sex and marriage. With the wind of some bizarre Supreme Court rulings at their backs (holding that the law may reflect irreligion but not religion), the gay activists have reason for optimism.

The supporters of traditional marriage should not underestimate what is at stake. Whether the gay activists know it or not, they are poised to destroy not just discrimination against homosexuals, but marriage itself. Outwardly, the advocates of gay marriage claim to admire marriage. But to claim the authority to redefine marriage, they must first claim that marriage is a flawed, man-made, institution that needs to be reworked; or worse yet, that it is merely a result of the unguided evolutionary process. Do not miss what is happening here. In order to gain the right of gay marriage, its advocates must first strip marriage of all transcendence, destroying the very thing that makes marriage lovely.

Gay activists claim to believe marriage is so meaningful that it should be extended to gays, but their case rests on the belief that marriage is so meaningless that it can be claimed by anyone who wants it. They say they want to broaden marriage to extend its joys to more people, but if marriage is expanded to encompass all committed, affectionate relationships, it will lose all of its meaning. This is the ultimate goal: to wrest marriage out from under God's authority, to destroy it, and to remake it to man's own liking. The power of a rebellious government is being used to do it. Christians need to understand what is at stake.

Part IV

The Plight of the Christian in a Hostile Society

★ CHAPTER 9 ★

Fear God, Honor the King

Where does all of this leave the Christian citizen? It leaves him with some very difficult questions. "Where is my place in civil society? How should I conduct myself as a citizen?" These are some of the most difficult questions that a thoughtful Christian will ask himself. Fortunately, there are some solid biblical answers, though they are not always the answers Christians like to hear.

Christians as Model Citizens

First and foremost, the Christian's posture toward earthly government should almost always be one of submission. In the second half of Romans, the Apostle Paul exhorts his Roman readers to selflessness and humility. This, Paul teaches, is the proper response to the knowledge of our own sinfulness, and of Christ's offer of salvation by faith. Paul tells the Roman Christians to put away their pride. He tells them to submit to their fellow believers and to take their place in the Body of Christ. He exhorts them to love others sincerely, even their enemies. He even instructs his fellow Christians, who were living under severe persecution by the Roman authorities, to submit to them. Paul then brings it all to a fine point:

> Let every person be subject to the governing authorities.... *not only to avoid God's wrath but also for the sake of conscience.* For because of this you also pay taxes, for the authorities are ministers of God, attending to this very thing. Pay to all what is owed to them: taxes to whom taxes are owed, revenue to whom revenue is owed, respect to whom respect is owed, honor to whom honor is owed.[1]

At first it is difficult to believe that Paul could mean what he says. It is tempting to conclude he was addressing a very narrow set of cultural circumstances and that his words were not intended as guidance for all Christians in all nations. Consider the words of the Apostle Peter, however, which he wrote to Christians scattered throughout many churches in diverse nations under different governments:

> *Be subject for the Lord's sake to every human institution*, whether it be to the emperor as supreme, or to governors as sent by him to punish those who do evil and to praise those who do good. For this is the will of God, that by doing good you should put to silence the ignorance of foolish people. Live as people who are free, not using your freedom as a cover-up for evil, but living as servants of God. Honor everyone. Love the brotherhood. Fear God. *Honor the emperor.*[2]

Both apostles urge obedient submission to earthly authorities. Even though God, in His sovereignty, has allowed Satan to have limited (but significant) control over the affairs of men,[3] and even though Scripture indicates some nations are under the charge of demons or of Satan himself,[4] Peter and Paul agree that the prevailing attitude of Christians toward their government should be one of submission. How can this be? Why should Christians submit to authorities that are in rebellion against God? Because, as Paul says earlier in Romans, there is no authority except that which God has established.[5] In other words, government is a divine institution. To disobey it to disobey an authority that God has established.

Government is Established by God

God created Heaven and the Earth and all of mankind. It was God, not man, who established government on Earth; and it was established to achieve God's purpose of restraining evil after the Fall. God delegates government authority to human beings. Therefore, human rulers, whether or not they are Christians, and whether or not their people are Christians, will answer to God and should seek His wisdom in ruling. But because civil authority is delegated to sinful people, government often becomes the source of oppression. In fact, "Throughout history, government has proved to be the chief instrument for thwarting man's liberty."[6]

Because we are familiar with sinful governments, even evil ones, it is difficult to believe that God established all of them. Yet this is the biblical teaching. The sovereign God establishes all nations and all authorities. It was God who appointed Abraham to be the father of the nation of Israel. Later, God appointed Moses and Aaron to lead that nation. Upon the death of Moses, God appointed Joshua to lead Israel into Canaan. When Joshua died, the Lord raised up a series of judges to lead Israel (some for better, some for worse). Eventually, when the nation of Israel had violated the covenant with God in nearly every possible way, the people called upon God for a king, and He begrudgingly established one by appointing Saul. Later, God personally chose David to govern Israel. And so on.

This is not only true for Israel. God is sovereign over the affairs of all other nations, too. The book of Job tells us "He makes nations great, and he destroys them; he enlarges nations, and leads them away."[7] Sometimes God uses one nation to judge another.[8] He even used other nations to judge the nation of Israel, His chosen people, by raising up hostile leaders to invade or enslave them.[9] To the Pharaoh who had enslaved the Jews and freed them only after God sent ten plagues upon Egypt, God said "For this purpose I have raised you up, to show you my power, so that my name may be proclaimed in all the earth."[10] When Jesus stood before Pontius Pilate, Jesus did not answer several of his questions. In frustration, Pilate asked him the seemingly rhetorical question, "You will not speak to me? Do you not know that I have authority to release you and authority to crucify you?" But to Jesus, the question was not a rhetorical one. He responded, "You would have no authority over me unless it had been given you from above."[11]

God is sovereign, and He sits above all government authorities. Government rulers must therefore answer to

God, and He will do justice in His own time. Even when Christians rightfully disagree with those authorities, Christians must maintain a posture of submission. Christians need not admire their rulers, but they must show appropriate honor. God has established their offices, and to dishonor them is to dishonor God. It is a matter of conscience.

In fact, to dishonor our rulers is in some ways a rebuke to God, because it implies that God's justice, whatever it may be and whenever it will be delivered, will not be sufficient for us.

In a world that operates on pride and savors rebellion, Christians are to be law-abiding people. Scanning all of Scripture, we find several accounts of prophets and apostles who were tried or jailed for preaching the Word of God, but find no instances of prophets or apostles being punished for mere civil misconduct. The only offense of the Christian against society should be the natural offense of living a life for God.

Where did Paul and Peter get these teachings on submission? No doubt they were influenced by the Old Testament passages mentioned above, and by the Mosaic Law given to the Jews by God, which contained harsh and sometimes public punishments for civil misconduct.[12] But Jesus himself reinforced those Old Testament lessons. Although modern liberal scholars have conjured the idea that Jesus was a political rebel, there is no record of Jesus defying the civil authorities. He spoke little about social injustice. He expended no energy wrestling with the oppressive and immoral Roman government, and He never lobbied for social reform. He taught that all men should pay taxes to the civil authorities, even corrupt ones.

When Jesus taught that men should render unto Caesar that which is Caesar's, He was standing within the decadent welfare state that was the Roman Empire. The taxes collected from Roman workers were used to support the elites and to fund pagan temples. Although Jesus had harsh words for the Pharisees and ransacked the temple on at least one occasion, He taught His disciples to obey the corrupt religious rulers by paying their temple tax.[13] These were taxes paid to the temple rulers who would ultimately call for His execution. Jesus was deferential, even submissive, to Herod and Pilate, as they presided over the kangaroo court that resulted in His crucifixion on charges Pilate knew were false.

From the example of Jesus and the apostles, we learn that Christians are to be compliant citizens—even when persecuted and even when rulers are openly corrupt. This guiding principle of submission to authority is something that marks the mature Christian and makes him different from anything the world has ever seen. Though trends within modern Christianity encourage edginess and crass, culturally-hip, and rebellious attitudes, mature Christians are not rebellious people. They do not recoil at authority or authority structures. To the contrary, because the mature Christian knows all authorities have been established by his Father in heaven—even the bad ones—his first instinct should be to submit and obey.

Promises from God vs. Promises from Men

In addition to the general rule of submission, there is another scriptural truth that informs the behavior and attitude of the mature Christian citizen. This is one of those truths that is learned not by its repetition in Scripture, but by its conspicuous absence from Scripture. Nowhere in the Bible are Christians promised a Christian government, nor even a government that honors God. In America, which was founded squarely on Christian principles, it is easy for Christians to feel as if they have been deprived of something owed to them, and those feelings can give birth to anger and malice. In many ways, American Christians have indeed been cheated; but they have been cheated by sinful man, not by God. God never promised that America would be a Christian country, a strong country, or even a good country. While it is heart-wrenching to witness the decline of America as she rejects her founding principles—the very principles of freedom—Christians should know it is bound to happen. Again, freedom rests on biblical truth, and in a fallen world, biblical truth is under constant assault. Understanding the Fall means accepting its reality.

Jesus hated sin, but it never shocked Him. He was never taken aback by man's depravity and foolishness because He knew all about it. He knew the full depth and breadth of the Fall, which is why He condescended to die for our sin in the first place. Christians who believe in the Fall understand it, too. In truth, the only really shocking thing is why America has not deteriorated sooner and faster.

All this is not as pessimistic as it may sound. Christians are not to sit by and watch society crumble with an "I told you so" attitude. Because God is sovereign and keeps His own counsel, Christians cannot know with certainty what the future holds for the West or for America. And because Christians take an eternal view, their behavior and attitudes should change little in good times and in bad. Christians do not know God's plan for society, but they know they are to stand for God's truth regardless of the circumstances and regardless of the consequences. Taking a stand for truth becomes more difficult in a culture that rejects it; but, again, God never promised His people a rose garden—not in this life, anyway.

If man's only hope were for redemption through government, pessimism would indeed be in order. For we know that government does not possess the power to reverse the Fall. It cannot deliver utopia. No law, rule, or scientific discovery can heal the heart of man.

> The delusion of the mechanical perfectibility of man through a combination of scientific knowledge and unconscious evolution has been responsible for much heartbreak. It is, at bottom, far more pessimistic than Christian pessimism, because, if science and progress break down, there is nothing to fall back upon. Humanism is self-contained—it provides for man no resources outside himself.[14]

But for all those who trust in Christ Jesus, there is a hope that is more certain than any promise from men and any dream of utopia. Jesus has the power to overcome the power of sin in our hearts, and secure our destiny in Heaven. And these promises, which He makes to all people of all nations on an individual basis, hold true under any government in any age. As for our nation, because we do not have access to God's plans, there is at least hope that He might move in a miraculous way to ease or reverse its decline.

When to Take Your Stand

Jesus' interaction with Pilate in the hours prior to His crucifixion was poignant. After Jesus was arrested, He was bound and brought before various religious and civil authorities. Several times when they questioned Him, He responded, but He never mounted a defense against the bogus charges. And the charges were obviously bogus. Even Pilate, the civil governor who reluctantly ordered Jesus' execution, did not find Jesus guilty. He ordered the execution for fear of the mob that was clamoring for Jesus' life.

Jesus came to Earth to die for the sin of mankind. He had come to terms with His mission. He had accepted the cup His Father had given Him. Although He answered a few questions at various stages in His show-trial, He was mostly silent. The only time He spoke with an assertive tone was when Pilate wrongly claimed that he possessed the authority to let Jesus live or die. "Do you not know that I have authority to release you and authority to crucify you?"[15] As noted earlier, although Jesus had been flogged nearly to death and had been silent in the face of other questions, He chose to correct Pilate. "You would have no authority over me at all unless it had been given you from above."[16] Jesus was going to die and knew it, but Pilate's claim of autonomous authority was such a destructive lie that Jesus could not let the moment pass without correcting the record.

Like Jesus, Christians should feel burdened to speak out against false claims of authority. When leaders claim authority over God, or apart from God, the Christian must attempt to correct the record. When leaders use their power to overrule God's clearly revealed truth, or to redefine it, Christians must take a stand. Christians should stand against any rule, law, or policy the government uses to substitute a lie for God's truth.

For example, when supporters of abortion rights use government to promulgate the lie that a fetus is not human, Christians should be moved to correct the record. Christians should stand for the biblical truth that unborn children are human beings created by the hand of God. Our affable friend from Chapter 2 may respond, "But not everyone believes the fetus is a creation of God!" And the Christian should reply, "Exactly! Now you are starting to understand." Pro-choicers believe the Bible is telling a lie. Pro-lifers believe the Bible is telling the truth. Both sides believe the other is pushing a lie about God, and both are fighting to have the law reflect their own view of reality—their beliefs about what God has said and has not said about unborn children.

The same can be said of gay marriage. The Bible teaches that God created marriage for one man and one woman. Many people today want the government to declare the biblical definition of marriage a lie. Both sides believe the other is pushing a lie about what God has said or has not said about marriage, and both want the law to reflect their belief. This struggle over whose beliefs should be reflected in the law has a name—it is called Democracy.

Secularists often claim to champion Democracy, but in truth, they are scared to death of it. Because Democracy involves the struggle to discern truth and to find reasonable laws that reflect the truth, Christians are well suited to participate in the public square, even one that is hostile to truth. Their primary focus should be to remind leaders that their authority comes from God and is constrained by God. Christians should eagerly vote, and should enjoy their rights to free speech and free assembly. In keeping with the general attitude of submission, however, they must do so only in ways that are becoming of a follower of Christ—that reflect love for their neighbors and their enemies.

When to Disobey the Ruling Authorities

There are, however, exceptions to the Christian's duty of submission. As indicated earlier, those exceptions are extremely narrow. Christians may rightfully disobey the civil authorities by employing proper biblical civil disobedience. The Bible teaches that Christians should—in fact, must—disobey the law when (1) the law requires them to do something that is forbidden by God's Word, or (2) the law forbids them from doing something God's Word commands them to do.

Scripture gives us several examples of appropriate civil disobedience. In Exodus, the Jewish midwives Shiphra and Puah were ordered by Pharaoh to kill all of the male Hebrew babies as they were born. The Bible says that

Shiphra and Puah feared God, however, and disobeyed Pharaoh's direct command. Because they refused to obey a decree from the king that would have forced them to violate God's commandment against murder, God blessed them.[17]

Similarly, Daniel and his friends Shadrach, Meshach, and Abednego, while enslaved in Babylon, were commanded to eat from the king's table. But they refused to obey the king's command, most likely because they did not wish to break the Mosaic dietary laws God had given the Hebrews. They were greatly blessed by God as a result. Later, Daniel's three friends were commanded to worship the golden images erected by King Nebuchadnezzar or face death in a blasting furnace. They refused to obey the king's command, even in the presence of the king himself, because God forbids His people to worship idols. The three boys were thrown into the fiery furnace, but were miraculously saved.[18]

After Daniel had risen to a position of prominence in the court of King Darius, his political enemies conceived a plan to remove him from power. They knew Daniel prayed to God daily, so they convinced the king to pass a law prohibiting prayer to anyone but the king. When Daniel continued to bow and pray to God in open defiance of the new law, he was thrown into the lion's den, and was famously spared by the hand of God.[19]

In the book of Acts, we read that Peter and John were twice ordered by the local Jewish authorities in Jerusalem not to teach in the name of Jesus. but they eagerly and happily disobeyed that directive, and were later thrown into jail.[20] Following these examples, Christians should disobey the law only when the conflict with God's law is clear, and only with careful consideration and prayer. Once the decision is made, the Christian must accept the punishment for his actions, whatever that punishment may be. When conscience requires a Christian to break a law, break it he must, but he must then accept without resistance the punishment he receives from the ruling authorities. It is shameful for a Christian who has acted boldly and honorably in civil disobedience to then try to escape the consequences. If God miraculously spares him from punishment as He sometimes did in the biblical examples above, he should count himself blessed. But remember, all of the apostles were imprisoned at some point in their ministries, and most were ultimately executed, but we have no record of any of them trying to escape the penalty for their actions.

When Paul was arrested in Jerusalem for preaching the Gospel (which led to a near riot in and around the temple), he told the governor, "If then I am a wrongdoer and have committed anything for which I deserve to die, I do not seek to escape death."[21] While Paul availed himself of his right as a Roman citizen to appeal his case to Caesar, nowhere do we read of Paul or any other apostle behaving flippantly, disrespectfully, or self-righteously.

Christian Activism—Some Warnings

All Christians know at least one dear, obedient, Christian who borders on what might be called a *political activist;* and at least one dear, obedient, Christian who shows no interest in politics, government, or current affairs of any kind. Perhaps you fall into one of those categories. There is indeed room in the Christian Church for both kinds of people; but both are bound by many of the same biblical parameters of Christian behavior: they must pray for their leaders, good and bad; they must resist idolatry of government and culture; they must seek to love their neighbors, and even their enemies; they must keep in mind the biblical separation of Church and state, resisting any temptation toward theocracy; and they must behave with decorum and dignity as representatives of Christ.

In the world of politics and public policy, there are many pitfalls the Christian must avoid. The chief pitfall for the Christian activist is the temptation to abandon the biblical view of the separation of Church and state. When the Christian sees depravity and self destruction all around, it is tempting to want to use state power to enforce Christian behavior. But Christians must remember that God has not given the state any power to change or heal the human heart. It is no substitute for the Holy Spirit; and when the state behaves badly, or when it is downright evil, Christians must console themselves with the knowledge that vengeance is the Lord's, and the Lord's alone.[22]

America's Founding Fathers were explicit in their reliance on Christian doctrines, but the Christian activist must be careful not to confuse the goals, hopes, and aspirations of the Founders with the promises of God in the Bible. God never promised that America would always respect Christianity. God never promised that America would remain free. While these things are clearly good for America, and worth supporting, Christians must be careful they do not confuse which promises came from which source. God's promises are always sure. Man's political promises are never sure.

The Christian activist must also take care that he does not make an idol of his political cause. It is easy for a person who cares deeply about politics to develop a "sky is falling" attitude toward government and particular leaders. We can begin to believe that a bad decision by the Supreme Court, or a disagreeable election result, has thwarted God's purposes and plans. Conversely, when there is a good decision by the Supreme Court, or an agreeable election outcome, the activist may feel a false sense of security that God's plan is back on track. This is getting dangerously close to idolatry, because God has not promised any particular government policy to Americans. Government policy is not God's instrument for saving souls or for redeeming His creation. God's instruments for saving souls are the Gospel of Christ and the Church, and regardless of how bad things get, His plan for His creation is not being thwarted.

Biblical righteousness always comes from the inside out. While good outward behavior can be good for the peace and stability of society—which is almost always a good thing—the Christian life cannot be focused on bringing society into biblical obedience through government power. God's plans do not rise and fall with the fortunes of any political party or court ruling. Christians are not released from their obligations to love their enemies, even when their enemies are deconstructing God's truth. Christians are to be faithful Christians no matter what type of government is in place. God never promised His people a Christian government, a just government, or a government that respects Christianity. Christians should be able to lose a political struggle—any political struggle—and not be shaken to the core. They must love their neighbor, even if their neighbor is a deconstructionist.

Loving Your Neighbor vs. Loving Your Neighborhood

The final warning for the Christian activist, which is closely related to the first two warnings, is to avoid the temptation of yearning for a Christian utopia. Amidst the teaching on community that is so popular in the Church today, there is much talk of *renewing* our communities and *transforming* our neighborhoods. The Church can in many ways be a blessing, not only to believers, but to unbelievers. But when Christians begin believing that the Church has a role to play in renewing or transforming our communities, they can fall into a very old and very dangerous pattern of thinking. They can slide toward a "social Gospel," in which the Church's primary purpose is not to save souls but to improve society. Christians must proceed with great caution here. When this view is fully embraced, the salvation of the individual is no longer an end in itself, but a means to an allegedly more important goal: the improvement of the society around them. This is simply a Christian version of the same utopian urge that has gripped the broader society.

Jesus never viewed the individual as a means to an end, not even the admirable end of a better society. He commanded His followers to "love your neighbor," not to "love your neighborhood." You can enjoy your neighborhood, have feelings of loyalty toward it, even prefer it to others; but you cannot love it as you can love a person made in the image of God. When your goal is to love a place or a community, each individual shrinks in importance, and your love has no specific person as its object. To love a person means to see them in the image of God. To love a place or a community usually bespeaks a desire to recreate it to fit your own desires. The goal of creating a community to your own liking—your very own heaven on Earth—is an evil one, even if done in the name of Jesus. The Christian's version of utopia may look very different than the secular one, but it is a utopian error nonetheless, originating from the same misconception of the Fall.

When Church leaders place a disproportionate emphasis on changing or saving communities, cities, or society in general, Church resources are misdirected and Christians can lose their focus on saving souls.[23] E.M. Bounds identifies this tendency as a temping scheme of Satan:

> One of [Satan's] devices is to pervert the aims of the church. He deludes church leaders into thinking that the main purpose of the church today is not so much to save individuals out of society as to save society, not so much to save souls as to save the bodies of men, not so much to save men out of a community as to save men and manhood in the community. The world, not the individual, is the subject of redemption.[24]

Bounds argues that the Church is like a net cast into the sea—not in order to change the sea, but to catch the fish out of the sea.[25] If a fisherman spent all of his energy trying to alter the chemical makeup of the sea in hopes of devising a way to catch more fish, he could spend his whole life at this task with little to show for his efforts.

In other words, any change or renewal experienced by a community is an *effect*, not the *purpose*, of a biblical ministry to *individuals* within that community. Christians are to be fishers of men, not captains of the culture. Cultural change in favor of God can result only after many individual conversions to Christ. Should Christians fight to change ungodly laws and tendencies that are common in our culture and which do harm (spiritual and physical) to people? Of course. It is only natural for Christians to seek truth and justice, even in an unbelieving world. But is it the *goal* of the Church to change *this world*, which will not survive the Second Coming? No. It should be the goal of the Church, rather, to save and help sanctify everlasting souls. The effects on society or the community are always secondary.

Perhaps most significantly, the talk of *renewal* of communities in the Church today is presumptuous. At its worst, it is Christian narcissism. Some Christians want their communities to reflect their values so they will be more comfortable there. They are understandably tired of feeling like aliens and outcasts from the culture, and they yearn to be more at home in their communities. Although Christians talk a lot about *renewal*, few pastors or writers ever define exactly what they mean. The reason they do not define what they mean is that they have no idea. The

Bible does not tell us what God's plan for our community might be. His plan might be to bring great revival to your city, as He did in the evil city of Nineveh after the people repented in response to the message delivered by the prophet Jonah. Or, God's plan might be to bring great destruction and suffering to your city, as He did to Nineveh several years later (and as He did to Jerusalem in 70 A.D.). When Christians embark on a great campaign to *renew* their community, they must first posit a vision of what that community should look like once they are done. But how do they know? How do they know God's plan? How can they divine His ways and His methods to accomplish His plans? Better to stick with the simpler missions actually given to the Church by God: to preach the Word, to make disciples, and to love our neighbors as ourselves.

This is an area of great temptation in the Church today. The Christian activist must take care that he doesn't substitute his own plan, and his own vision, for the Lord's. He must also take care that he doesn't commit the same error that is being committed by secular society: a distortion of the proper roles of Church and state. He must keep things in proportion. Above all, he must remember that his fundamental posture toward the ruling authorities is submission. He must pray for his leaders and give due honor to the offices they hold.

And most importantly, he needs to remember that God never promised him a free country, a prosperous country, or even a rational government. If anything, God warns the Christian that he is an alien in this world, and that this world will reject him and his beliefs. To pine for heaven and to yearn for Christ's return in glory are the special jewels of Christian hope. But to wish for a different world this side of heaven is to wish for that which God has not ordained—it is a wish that God would do things differently. This is a dangerous wish.

Warnings to the Apolitical Christian

The apolitical Christian faces pitfalls as well. He might become so cynical about government, so uninterested in politics, that he begins to view himself above the fray. He may convince himself that nothing matters except ministry, failing to see that loving your neighbor sometimes requires him to take a public stand for God's truth. Ironically, if you think government and politics are too worldly for you, or that they are beneath you, you may be falling into the classic secular mistake of believing that government is wholly separate from God and God's authority.

Perhaps most importantly, the apolitical Christian should examine his heart to determine why he is apolitical. He must make sure that he is not overly concerned with what others think of him. Is he shying away from a public identification with Christ, the Bible, or truth? Is he desperate to disassociate himself from his fellow believers? We must not be cowed by the fear of men. Standing for the truth in a fallen world is difficult. The world will disapprove. Persecution by unbelievers— even by some who claim to be Christians—will follow. If the apolitical Christian shrinks from battle for fear of being identified publicly with Jesus, he must regroup and remember who he is. Christ was hated, and He warned His followers that they, too, would be hated. When we want to be loved by the very world that rejected our Lord, we are seeking to be greater than He is. We may desire His grace and forgiveness without the consequences that accompany His truth. This desire to have it both ways drew a sharp warning from Jesus that reverberates down through the ages:

> A disciple is not above his teacher, nor a servant above his master. It is enough for the disciple to be like his teacher, and the servant like his master. If they have called the master of the house Beelzebub, how much more will they malign those of his household.[26]

ENDNOTES

1   Romans 13:1, 5-7 (emphasis added)

2   1 Peter 2:13-17 (emphasis added)

3   See 1 John 5:19; John 12:31, 16:11, 14:30.

4   In Daniel 10, the "Prince of the Kingdom of Persia" is described as a supernatural being. Isaiah identifies the earthly king of Babylon with the "star of the morning" and the "son of the dawn," which are also references to Satan. See Isaiah 14:4-12; Ezekiel 28:12-14.

5   Romans 13:2

6   Barry M. Goldwater, *The Conscience of a Conservative*, reprinted 2007 by BN Publishing, p. 10.

7   Job 12:23

8   See the long list of nations that God punished by using other nations to invade or enslave them, Jeremiah 45-51.

9   See, e.g., Isaiah 10:5-11; and Jeremiah 24.

10 Exodus 9:16. See also Romans 9:17.

11 John 19:10-11

12 See Deuteronomy 19:13.

13 Matthew 17:24-27

14 Sayers, p. 46.

15 John 19:10

16 John 19:11

17 Exodus 1:7

18 Daniel 3:16-18

19 Daniel 6:7

20 Acts 4:17-18, 5:27-29

21 Acts 25:11

22 Romans 12:19

23 I would add that a mission to save or renew our society is so vague
    a mission that most individuals cannot possibly grasp it. Bounds
    predicts that the church whose leaders expend their resources trying
    to change their community will "lose sight of spiritual edification" as
    a primary purpose of the Church. E.M. Bounds, *Guide to Spiritual
    Warfare*, p. 56.

24 E.M. Bounds, *Guide to Spiritual Warfare*, p. 52.

25 E.M. Bounds, *Guide to Spiritual Warfare*, p. 54.

26 Matthew 10:24-25

CHAPTER 10

Render Unto Caesar

Then the Pharisees went and plotted how to entangle him in his words. And they sent their disciples to him, along with the Herodians, saying, "Teacher, we know that you are true and teach the way of God truthfully, and you do not care about anyone's opinion, for you are not swayed by appearances. Tell us, then, what you think. Is it lawful to pay taxes to Caesar, or not?" But Jesus, aware of their malice, said, "Why put me to the test, you hypocrites? Show me the coin for the tax." And they brought him a denarius. And Jesus said to them, "Whose likeness and inscription is this?" They said, "Caesar's." Then he said to them, "Therefore render to Caesar the things that are Caesar's, and to God the things that are God's." When they heard it, they marveled. And they left him and went away. (Matthew 22:15-22)

This is one of the classic traps set for Jesus by His detractors. Note, however, that this was a plot between the Pharisees and the Herodians. The Herodians, as their name indicates, supported Rome and King Herod. The Pharisees did not support Rome and were antagonistic to King Herod. These two groups were normally at loggerheads, but joined forces under the ancient theory that the enemy of my enemy is my friend. Jesus was their mutual enemy.

They knew that if Jesus said it was right to pay taxes to Caesar, He would have been confirming Caesar as the true authority in Israel, which would have greatly offended the Pharisees. And if Jesus said it was wrong to pay taxes to Caesar, He would have been advocating the breaking of Roman law, which would have offended the Herodians.

Jesus responded by pointing to a denarius they showed Him, and asking a rhetorical question, "Whose likeness and inscription is this?" Of course, everyone knew that Caesar's image and inscription were imprinted on the coin. So Jesus told them the answer to their riddle: "Therefore render to Caesar the things that are Caesar's, and to God the things that are God's."

The Scripture then says that the Pharisees and Herodians who had set the trap for Jesus "marveled" at His answer and went away. Why did they marvel? They marveled because Jesus had reached behind their question and exposed their worldly motivations.

These two groups, the Pharisees and Herodians, were locked in a struggle for power over Israel. Political power had become their goal. They were all citizens of Israel, the nation created by God for great works, but they had become so consumed with their political circumstances that they lost sight of what was truly important to God.

Worldly power was their greatest aspiration. Jesus would turn their thinking upside down.

This teaching by Jesus is cited the world over as a statement about Jesus' view of money and taxes. While this passage does tell us to "render unto Caesar" the taxes that are due, this teaching is about much more than money and taxes. When He asked them "whose likeness and inscription is on the coin," the Jews who were listening would have immediately made the connection between Jesus' words and Genesis 1:27, describing God's creation of Adam and Eve: "So God created man in His own image; in the image of God he created him."

Jesus was telling the people to render unto Caesar that which bears Caesar's image—their money, their taxes—but to render unto God that which bears God's image—their very selves. He was essentially telling them, "In your daily affairs, by all means pay to Caesar those taxes which he collects by his worldly authority. He minted the coinage. He governs the economy. If he orders you to pay taxes, then you should pay your taxes. But while you are so consumed with exactly who owes what to whom, remember that God made something that bears His likeness as well—YOU! And while you are rendering your tax obligations to Caesar, render also your obligations to your Creator, by giving Him your very life. Give your coins to Caesar, but give your life to God."

Jesus did not denigrate Caesar's authority. He was affirming the importance of government because it plays such a large role in determining our circumstances. But He also reminds us that there is always something more important than our circumstances: the condition of our hearts. It is good to work to improve the circumstances in which we live. But as Christians, we know there is a more important struggle going on in the world—the struggle to bring the truth of God to the human heart. The government has no power to change a human heart. God's instrument for changing hearts is not the government, but the Church, the Body of Christ on Earth, spreading the Gospel message and living the Gospel life amidst a fallen world. We know that when God's Word goes out into the world, it will not return void. And we know that the Church need have no fear, for even the gates of hell will not prevail against it.

Thus, the Christian should have no desire to create heaven on Earth, for he knows there is a heaven already— in Heaven. He knows that this world is marked for destruction when Christ returns, which may be tomorrow or ten thousand years from now. His struggles here on Earth are not for power, not for cultural renewal, and not for control over the lives of others. His battle is not for this world. His battle is to help rescue individual people from this world. He sees in the example of Christ something far more glorious than an earthly victory for Christianity. He sees a heavenly one. This is the Christian's great secret. He is the only one who realizes that this world is passing away. He is the only one who understands that the soul, not the senate, is the greatest prize. He is the only one who, knowing all of this, is truly free to love his neighbor as himself.

The Final Victory

And so the Christian fights valiantly, though to all the world he appears to be losing the battle. But what appears as loss is really gain. His final victory is already secured. When Christ was falsely charged with blasphemy and brought before Herod and Pontius Pilate, He might have waved a hand and destroyed them. He might have won a great victory here on Earth to prove his Lordship, power, and strength for all to see. He might have wiped their kingdoms off the map and built a heavenly kingdom in their place, as His disciples eagerly expected Him to do. Instead, He stood quietly and allowed the forces of evil to temporarily overtake Him.

As Christ hung on the Cross, His battle also appeared to be lost. To those who prize earthly power, it still appears lost. But Christ was actually winning. What looked to mankind like a tragic defeat was actually a glorious victory. How can this be? How can Christ's crucifixion be a victory for Christ? How can defeat result in victory?

The key to the riddle lies in the fact that, while there is one war being waged between God and Satan, there are different battles being fought in different locations, for different purposes. Man is engaged in a mighty rebellion here on Earth to establish his own authority and build his own earthly kingdom. Men battle against God and among themselves for worldly power and riches. Christ was fighting a different battle in the same war. He did not fight for earthly political power because He knows such power is futile and temporary. He fought against sin, Satan, and death, here on our earthly battlefield; but His victory parade and spoils are elsewhere—in Heaven.

Christ appeared to be losing the battle here, but He was winning the war there. Christians are likewise embroiled in a worldly battle—which by all worldly measures is a losing one—but our victory and our spoils are elsewhere. We join with Christ in storing up the spoils of an eternal victory where they cannot be seen.

This is the essence of Christian faith. Christians can bear to lose the contest to rule the Earth, but they will fight like guerillas to save individual souls. We must never look at another person as a mere voter, or statistic, or an opportunity for power. We must instead see a living soul made in the image of God, who will spend eternity either in heaven or in hell. The world is a sinking ship. Our job is to give people the life raft of the Gospel, not to place our eternal hope in any plan to repair the ship. Our job is to be fishers of men—to share God's Word that alone has power to save men out of the depths and death of the ocean; not to spend all of our time, treasure, and talents seeking to make the ocean a more attractive place to live.

This is spiritual maturity: knowing that obedience to the Lord is an end in itself, even if the world is crumbling around you. We don't obey so that He will give us freedom or democracy. We don't obey to bring about a Christian utopia that God never promised. We don't obey to sustain a self-image of a good person. We don't obey to receive the admiration of others. And we don't obey to be saved—because our works cannot save us. We obey because Christ first loved us. We obey because we serve the King of Kings who desires that we be like Him. We obey because He teaches us to love His truth. And we obey because obedience to His commands is the only authentic expression of love for Him.

Christians must resist the desire to feel the rush of worldly victory—to see the world renewed to our liking now. That is simply not the calling of the Christian. Our calling is to stand firm here and now on the side of truth—against lies, against sin, against Satan—knowing we will not ultimately change this world, but knowing we will, by God's grace, point others to Christ and His glory. We do not love this world, and we do not seek to change it, but to overcome it, and to teach others that if Christ is their Savior, they too can overcome it.

Then one awful and glorious day, when the trumpet sounds and Christ returns to gather His people, to separate the sheep from the goats, to establish His throne among men and to make all things new—the government will be upon His shoulder.